Study Guide

Teacher Edition

~~~

Ye shall be as gods

Study Guide

Teacher Edition

~~~

Ye shall be as gods

Humanism and Christianity

~~~

The Battle for Supremacy in the American
Cultural Vision

Larry G. Johnson

Published by Anvil House Publishers, LLC
Owasso, Oklahoma
www.anvilhousebooks.com

Printed in the United States of America.
Cover: Whitley Graphics
Cover Photo: iStockphoto.com

ISBN: 978-0-9839716-1-0

Contents

The Value and Purpose of the Study Guide

The purpose of writing *Ye shall be as gods* was to diagnose and illuminate the causes of the cultural disquiet that is and has been pervasive in American life for the last half century. The book provides a comprehensive overview of the source of the anger, frustration, and sense of helplessness as Americans see the Judeo-Christian ethic upon which the nation was founded come under relentless attack in the institutions of American life. The Study Guide provides a distillation of those fundamental and compelling truths that were the basis of the American cultural vision. The Study Guide will:

- Give an understanding of the tenets and tactics of humanism and the failure of the humanistic worldview to answer the basic questions of life.

- Equip Christians with definitive answers in the battle of worldviews as they work toward renewing and restoring the culture.

- Increase faith as the reader understands the Bible is the source of the infallible truth of God for all of mankind and for all time.

- Provide prescriptive remedies necessary to counteract humanism's unrelenting assault on the American cultural vision.

The Study Guide may be used by groups or individuals. The Teacher Edition provides questions and answers. The Student Edition provides questions with space to write answers. Both editions give the page numbers of the book where answers may be found to the questions posed. Sources of quotations and other reference material used in the Study Guide are not reproduced in the Study Guide. The location of these sources and reference material will be found on the pages of the book referred to in the Study Guide.

Part I – The Boomers

Introduction

1. In the last paragraph of the Introduction, what causes the author a sense of disquiet? (7-8)

It was the face of the generation of which he was a member that had changed during two tumultuous years he had been away in the late 1960s. The unidentified stirrings within the author's mind that something was amiss became the subject of his book over four decades later. That subject would be the ascendency of the humanistic worldview and its eventual domination of the institutions of American life.

Chapter 1 – The Baby Boomers – Growing Up

1. What are the birth years and size for the Greatest Generation, Silent Generation, and Boomers? (10-11)

The G.I. generation, now called the Greatest Generation, was born from 1901 through 1924 (24 years and 63 million members). The Silent generation was born from 1925 through 1942 (18 years and 49 million members). Strauss and Moore placed the beginning of the Boomer generation in 1943 and ending at the close of 1960. For purposes of this book, we shall generally consider the Boomers to be those born between the end of 1945 and the end of 1964 (19 years and 79 million members).

2. What are the characteristics of the three generations? (10)

Greatest Generation - Called the "civic" types and described as believers in public harmony, cooperative social discipline, friendly, optimistic, and having community spirit. Silent Generation - Other-directed, adaptive, fair, open-minded, and non-judgmental. Boomer Generation - Idealists with unyielding opinions about all issues and exceptionally judgmental.

3. What shapes the consciousness of an entire generation? (11)

1

Karl Manheim stated that early impressions tend to coalesce into a natural view of the world. Others would restate Manheim's "decisive events and impressions" by referring to a generational cohort who grew up and came of age together and "…shared experiences during formative years that have a common and lasting effect on values and lifestyle decisions of a group of people." The author summarized the definitions of those things that give face to a generation as *significant shared events and formative experiences.*

4. The significant shared events and formative experiences of the Boomers resulted in dramatic changes in what areas of American life? (11)

Family life, child rearing, education, culture, religion, politics, and government.

5. The Boomers' first two significant shared events and formative experiences were most influenced by which two men and in what areas of American life? (11)

Benjamin Spock in child rearing and John Dewey in education.

6. Why was Benjamin Spock so important in forming the Boomers' worldview? (11-12, 21)

Within the first year Boomers were born, Spock published his *Common Sense Book of Baby and Child Care*. Released in the spring of 1946, three quarters of a million copies were sold by year's end. His influence on child rearing in America and around the world cannot be overestimated. One poll found that almost two-thirds of new mothers had read *Baby and Child Care* in the late 1940s and 1950s.

7. How did Spock's approach to child rearing impact the Boomer generation and those that followed? (16, 21)

Caroline Zachry, a New York Psychoanalytic Institute member and educator/psychologist at Columbia, encouraged Spock in developing his child-rearing methods. Zachry embraced Sigmund Freud's theories and the views of Columbia's John Dewey on childhood development. These views were anti-traditionalist and challenged memorization and rigid discipline in school. Rather, the individual child should determine the curriculum as opposed to an administrator. The primary purpose of school was to teach children how to cooperate and get along and in the world. Contrary to Calvinists and behaviorists, Spock's book offered a progressive philosophical view of children as essentially good at heart, not little villains or formless lumps of clay waiting for impressions. Spock applied the principles found in psychoanalysis throughout his book, and of all the experts relied upon, Freud would exert the largest influence. By the end of the 1950s, America had also indirectly absorbed many of Freud's theories about human nature.

8. How did Spock's approach to discipline of children differ from the traditionalists' view? (17)

With regard to discipline, the psychoanalytic view of the individual conscience was reflected in Spock's book. Freud believed that mankind's brutish instincts were kept in check because people desired to be loved and get along in society. Likewise, Spock contended that, "The thing that keeps us from doing 'bad' things to each other is the feelings we have of liking people and wanting them to like us. In other words, if a child is handled in a friendly way, he wants to do the right thing, the grown-up thing, most of the time." Spock's emphasis is on discipline that is based on a child's desire to be good and get along in society, and he is very light on punishment.

9. What was the ultimate impact of Spock's philosophy in raising children? (20)

Spock's book would create a seismic shift away from the Judeo-Christian tradition and its doctrine of fallen man.

10. What two men influenced Spock's worldview the most, and what were those influences? (21)

By the end of the 1950s, America had also absorbed indirectly many of Freud's theories about human nature. Newspapers and magazine columns, among them Spock's monthly essays, offered a squeaky-clean version of Freud, the popularized 'American Freud,' a sanitized Freud who was the author of most of the gifts of liberal culture— liberal education, psychiatric social work, permissive child raising, modern psychology, and criminology. In addition to Freud, John Dewey's ideas on progressive education would strongly influence Spock.

11. What was the philosophy of John Dewey? (24-25)

The dominant theme or central idea of John Dewey's philosophy is human self-realization accomplished through interaction with nature. "In this consists man's happiness which is nothing less than the gradual development of man's capacities as he acts in and through nature." In this philosophy, nothing can be admitted which transcends the possibilities of concrete, human experience. There is no absolute, no transcendent being, no extra-mundane reality…there is no room for a supernatural religion…and that 'supernatural' means that which transcends the possibilities of concrete human experience and involves an absolute being." From this philosophical theme Dewey addressed art, education, morals, politics, science, and religion. The second central idea of Dewey's philosophy is democracy in education, "…an equality of concern for each individual in the community to develop himself as a person." Dewey's third central idea was that the ways human beings learn can be discovered through scientific psychological study.

12. How did John Dewey's humanistic philosophy capture American education? (25)

Psychology, published by Dewey in 1896, was the first American textbook on the "revised" subject of education. It became the most widely read, quoted, and used textbook in American schools of education. Beginning with his twenty-five-year affiliation with Columbia University's Teachers' College, Dewey's writings shaped the twentieth century U.S. curriculum. His ideas on education would extensively permeate American education, and the results are still being felt today.

Chapter 2 – Boomers – The Fifties

1. What was the Boomers' third significant shared event and formative experience and how did it become so significant? (28)

Television ownership would mushroom from one hundred thousand in 1948 to fifty million by 1959. Of all the wonders of TV, none was more remarkable than the speed with which it came. Television conquered America in less than a generation. Gutenberg's printing press would take five hundred years to reach its full impact. Only one household in one hundred had a television in 1948. The percentage of American homes having a television grew to nine percent within two years, sixty-five percent by 1955, and eighty-six percent by1959. By 1959, a majority of all Boomers had been born, and the oldest Boomer children were in their middle teens.

2. How did television impact family life? (28)

With the advent of television, there was a new member of the family. Television exposed the American child to substantial external influences for long periods of time each day.

3. What was television's impact on the larger culture outside of the home? (29)

As Michael Novak wrote, television became the "…molder of the soul's geography. It builds up incrementally a psychic structure of expectations. It does so in much the same way that school lessons slowly, over the years, tutor the unformed mind and teach it 'how to think'." Television is a "homogenizing medium" with an ideological tendency that is a "vague and misty liberalism" designed "however gently to undercut traditional institutions and to promote a restless, questioning attitude." It was television that gave a face to the Boomers' sense of generational identity and separated them from every past generation.

4. What were the Boomers' fourth significant shared event and formative experience and how did that experience and event make Boomers different from other generations? (30)

The fourth significant shared event and formative experience was the enormous size of the Boomer cohort in relation to the generations before and after it. The Boomer cohort was different from past generations because its size made it the single greatest demographic event in American history.

5. What effect did the size of the Boomer cohort have on them? (31-32)

Size of the Boomer cohort influenced the generation in two ways. First, they became a large market. Business was quick to capitalize on this huge market. By using television, marketers talked directly to Boomers, bypassing their parents. Second, Boomers also commanded attention in education. During the 1940s and 1950s, kindergarten through high school classrooms were being built and filled in record numbers. The growth at the college and university level would begin in the 1960s as Boomers moved into adulthood. Thus, because of their size, Boomers set the agenda in both education and the marketplace, and this gave them a sense of their generation's relative importance compared to their parents.

6. What were the events that caused American prosperity to become the fifth significant shared event and formative experience? (32)

First, the postponement of marriage and childbearing during the Great Depression and World War II that led to a bunching of family formation by this older group immediately after World War II. Second, this bunching occurred at the same time the younger service men and women returning from the war began family formations. Third, at the end of World War II America found itself at the pinnacle of world power, both militarily and economically. It was the sole nuclear power, and its lands and industry were untouched by the ravages of war. It was a giant nation full of natural resources. Therefore, a large population with pent-up demands and the resources to fulfill those demands resulted in a unique era of prosperity during the growing-up years of most Boomers.

7. How did this exceptionally prosperous era affect the Boomers? (32-33)

The starting point for Boomers was their shared expectations about the future, rooted in the robust economic growth of their formative years. They took for granted a world of unbridled economic optimism, unprecedented abundance, and wide-ranging prosperity. Boomers grew up with a presumption of economic security, and thus a sense that the future could be taken for granted and would assuredly turn out to be a brighter place than yesterday or today. The presumption of economic security and the taking for granted of continued economic optimism, abundance, and prosperity that would last forever created a new mindset in America—that of entitlement.

8. What was the Boomers' sixth significant shared event and formative experience and what caused it? (34)

The spectacular technological achievements of the late 1940s and 1950s significantly influenced the Boomers. These achievements were a continuation of the rapid technological advances of World War II. Although mostly of military orientation including the atom bomb, the technological advances did not slow following the war but shifted along more consumer-oriented paths.

9. List several of these technological achievements and discuss the reasons that one of those achievements is ranked as being most important. (34-36)

The significant technological achievements of the 1940s and 1950s include the atom bomb, transistor, antibiotics and other medical breakthroughs such as the polio vaccine, cracking the DNA code, jet travel, television, and the interstate highway system. The most important achievement was the launching of Sputnik I by the Russians in 1957 which resulted in massive investments by the United States in education and sparked the race to the Moon that became the centerpiece in the Cold War.

10. What was the attitude of many of the Boomers in the 1960s and 1970s with regard to their parents' generation and the decade of the 1950s? (37)

It became the accepted fashion among many Boomers and the institutions they represented to demean their parents' generation and the decade of the 1950s and to a lesser extent the late 1940s. Derogatory descriptions included their derisive denunciation of the era for its supposed willful authority and blind conformity, rigidity, hypocrisy, bigotry, repression, prudishness, and materialism to name a few.

11. How does the author rebut these charges? (37-40)

Willful Authority and Blind Conformity - These are the same men and women who were soldiers and sailors that sloughed through four years of combat in World War II. They stood up to the worst the enemy had to offer. They were fearless, focused on the mission, had a strong work ethic, and a healthy respect for authority. And they carried these qualities into the postwar workplace. It was normal for those men and women to work hard toward the accomplishment of the corporate mission. Thus, the better description of the 1950s American man and woman would be one of respect for authority and a focus on mission, not slavish obedience. (37-38)

Materialism - Many were children or young adults during the depravations of the Great Depression. Then along came World War II with millions living a Spartan soldier's life on the battle fronts of the world while those at home coped with shortages and rationing of goods and services. They came out of World War II much older and wiser than most generations beginning family life and working careers. Hard work and prosperity made it possible to own a home of their own, to drive a car of their own, have adequate food for their families, and with a little left over for some of life's simple pleasures. All of this catching up was crammed into a short ten to fifteen years as they approached middle age. (38-39)

Bigotry, racism, and repression - There was a measure of racism and repression as had there been in every generation since our founding. America's record has been far from perfect, but with each successive generation there was progress on achieving the nation's ideals regarding racial equality. It will never be achieved in one generation and, given the human condition, it may never be achieved completely. However, there was progress in the 1940s and 1950s in moving toward

8

the American ideals with regard to discrimination and racism. The progress made in the 1960s on race and poverty was a product of the 1950s generation that has been so maligned by the Boomers. (39-40)

Chapter 3 – Boomers – The Sixties – Ye shall not surely die

1. Describe the origins of the worldview of the Greatest Generation. (43)

The Greatest Generation's worldview was born in the cauldron of economic chaos and threats from maniacal despots attempting to enslave the world, and their worldview rested on their patrimony that was birthed in Western civilization.

2. Although President John Kennedy was a member of the Greatest Generation and shared that generation's worldview, how did his election and the 1960s in general differ from the 1950s? (43-44)

The election of Kennedy signaled a new era in America—an expectancy of something new, bright, young, and hopeful. At Kennedy's death in November 1963, the oldest Boomer was almost eighteen, and the last of the Boomers would be born only thirteen months later.

3. What is the stereotypical image of the Boomers and why is it not descriptive of the majority of the Boomer generation? (44)

The stereotypical TV image of the 1960s Boomer was and remains sex, drugs, rock 'n' roll, protest, rebellion, and dropping out. The protesters that fostered this image did not represent the majority of the people in their generation due to differences in lifestyles and values.

4. How were the Boomers divided with regard to lifestyles and values? (44-46)

In 2006 Yankelovich conducted an extensive study of the diversity of Boomer hopes, dreams, and aspirations. To accomplish the study Boomers were separated into discrete attitudinal groups, each with a distinctive set of first priorities. Straight Arrows are the most conservative, hold traditional values, consider religion as important and a source of comfort in life, have a strong sense of ethical clarity, and have the highest rejection of premarital sex and free-spirited nonconformity. At the other end of Boomer spectrum are the protesters described as radicals and activists which comprise less than one-sixth of the Boomers. The majority of this group has a liberal or radical orientation and rank highest in societal priorities and social causes. The other four attitudinal groups comprise the remaining half of the Boomers. Their values and priorities tend to fall between the two ends of the Boomer spectrum.

5. What are the radical/protester achievements of the Boomer culture claimed by Leonard Steinhorn? (47)

Boomer culture has embraced diversity, liberated women, demolished discriminatory barriers, democratized institutions, freed up individual expression, fought for a healthier environment, and annulled the shame of being different.

6. Discuss the myth of the Boomer generation's claim to be responsible for all of the great social and political revolutions of the 1960s. (48)

Boomers were merely the foot soldiers for change, not the catalysts. For the most part, 1960s Boomers merely adopted what others had conceived. Their numbers and enthusiasm behind those conceptions and made them important. Boomers had been conditioned and trained by the significant shared events and formative experiences of the late 1940s and the 1950s. But, members of prior generations were the true catalysts for revolution. For good or ill, the generals of the prior generations dictated the marching orders to the impressionable Boomer troops of the 1960s. As Croker wrote, "They (Boomers) just seemed to us to be such powerful agents of change that we can't help but blame them and credit them with things that probably were beyond their control."

7. What were the three broad currents of social and political change in the 1960s? (48)

Cultural change, race, and war.

8. What are the three significant areas of cultural change in the 1960s as described by the author? Summarize each. (48-50)

11

Sexual revolution – The great influx of women into the labor market and growth of single motherhood during the 1940s and the growth of pre-marital sex in the 1950s were foundational supports for the explosion of the sexual revolution of the 1960s. The development of the birth control pill in the early 1960s had a greater impact on attitudes regarding sex and conception as opposed to promoting sex through the actual usage of the pill. (48-49)

Changes in media and arts – New offerings in literature, books, film, stage, television, and music assaulted the boundaries of traditional morality. Three Supreme Court cases challenged and overturned existing obscenity laws: *Lady Chatterley, Tropic of Cancer*, and *Fanny Hill*. As a result of these cases, three tests to determine the presence of obscenity would thereafter be applied: was the appeal predominantly prurient, was it patently offensive, and was there an absence of serious social value? Unless a work failed all three tests, the First Amendment would prohibit suppression. (49)

Free Speech Movement – FSM's attack on a university's authority to control the speakers allowed on campus would ultimately result in vast changes to academic government, student rights, and a new definition of the university. The shock waves that spread from the FSM would merge with the civil rights movement and Vietnam anti-war protests and create cauldrons of rebellion on campuses across America in the middle and late 1960s and early 1970s. (50)

9. Describe the status of discrimination and equality in America during the 1940s and 1950s. (51)

Following World War II, prosperity had prompted a dramatic postwar drop in racial, religious, ethnic, and sexual discrimination.

10. Describe America's efforts at eliminating racial discrimination in the 1940s and 1950s. (51-52)

Color lines were broken in major sports in the late 1940s and early 1950s. By all prior standards, racial equality advanced significantly during World War II, the late 1940s, and during the decade of the 1950s. A number of the executive, legislative, and judicial actions were steadily tearing down the barriers to racial equality including the

Supreme Court decision that outlawed school segregation in 1954, the Civil Rights Act of 1964 that barred discrimination in public places and employment, and the Voting Rights Act of 1965 that removed obstacles to voting by blacks. The attitudes of Americans about race, religion, minorities, ethnic groups, and discrimination in general were changing for the better, and their change of attitudes was followed by action.

11. What were the subtle changes in the fight for equality in the early 1960s as described by the author, and what were the causes for this new view of equality? (52)

In the fight for equality, equality of condition and outcome were increasingly seen as essential for equality of opportunity. The first cause of this new view of equality was the civil rights movement of the 1960s. The excessive resistance to equal treatment before the law in the south produced a belief that equality could only be ended by political and judicial action. The second cause was a growing belief that equality of opportunity required a leveling of social conditions and as a consequence the importance of individual effort was devalued. The third cause was the changing definition of what constituted equality which resulted in courts becoming the arbiters of social policy.

12. What were the elements that hindered the progress toward racial equality, harmony, and brotherhood as espoused in Martin Luther King's "I have a dream" speech in 1963? (52-53)

Riots and destruction in dozens of American cities during the 1960s, the rise of the Black Power movement, the race hucksterism of some black and white politicians and civil rights leaders, and the ever growing governmental attempts at leveling society which ultimately leads to socialism with resulting declines in quality of life, standards of living, and loss of trust in government and its institutions.

13. Describe the fundamental difference in the approach to equality and morality between Martin Luther King and those holding the humanistic worldview. (53)

King believed the most fundamental basis for our republican form of government was a social contract made under the authority of a higher law, not simply a social contract between the people and those who govern. King espoused the Biblical moral code that flowed from the Biblical teachings of Jesus Christ. Humanists such as Steinhorn believed that, "…it was never enough to change policies or enact laws. They demanded that assumptions, norms, and attitudes change as well. However, King understood that attitudes and assumptions are changed through an acceptance of and adherence to those very norms Steinhorn would change, and therefore King rejected the imperious imposition of new norms.

14. What was the ultimate result of the quest for equality as opposed to a quest for racial harmony and brotherhood? (54-55)

Two results occurred as the nation embarked on a quest for equality through the efforts of thousands of politicians, judges, bureaucrats, and social engineers, each armed with a magnifying glass and carpenter's level. First, government resources are not adequate and never can be to achieve the levels of equality sought. Government cannot do everything for everybody. People and institutions must do some things for themselves. The perceived failure of government in insuring equality leads to less trust in government. Second, although Americans generally favor more fairness and equality in national life, their generosity weakens and shrinks when the government's efforts to help one group impinge on another.

15. Describe the geo-political domino theory and its application to South Vietnam. (58-59)

The domino theory was a subset of the larger containment policy that had been the basic U.S. strategy since the end of World War II for responding to Soviet military and political power in Europe and other communist-led movements in the world. President Eisenhower first espoused this theory in 1954 in describing the consequences of a loss by the French in its war in Vietnam. It was believed that if Vietnam fell under communist control, other countries in the region (Laos, Cambodia, and Thailand) would fall to communism. This was a continuation of the policy President Truman followed in aiding Greece and Turkey to prevent the spread of communist regimes in eastern Europe.

16. During America's involvement in the Vietnam, one year stands out as the epitome of the turmoil in America during the 1960s. Name that year and describe the events that defined the decade. (59)

On both the home front and in Vietnam, 1968 was a tumultuous year—peace marches, sit-ins, protests, college campuses in turmoil, assassinations of Martin Luther King and Robert Kennedy, riots at the Chicago Democratic National Convention, capture of an American ship (Pueblo) by North Korea and imprisonment of its crew, decision of Lyndon Johnson to not seek a second term as president, beginning of the Paris peace talks, Tet Offensive, My Lai Massacre, and riots that set aflame a hundred U.S. cities. (59)

17. What happened to the rebellious Boomers following the 1960s? (65-66)

Many of the rebellious Boomers who flirted with the protest movement and radical lifestyles eventually came back to the cultural home of their parents. But many of the unrepentant leaders of the rebellion would eventually assume positions of power and leadership in America and find new ways to challenge their cultural ancestry. The imposition of their worldview has changed America and its institutions, and much of that change is questionable.

Part II – Worldview

Chapter 4 – Worldview: Christianity vs. Humanism

1. Describe what is meant by "worldview." (70)

Worldview is the comprehensive framework of one's basic beliefs about things. Things include the world, human life, social morality, education, family, and God. Beliefs are claims to a certain kind of knowledge one is willing to defend, that is, those beliefs to which one is committed. In other words, beliefs have to do with one's convictions and matters of general principle. A worldview is a person's beliefs about the world that directs his or her decisions and actions.

2. Why must we concern ourselves with worldview? (70)

The beliefs one holds tend to create a pattern, design, or structure that fit together in a particular way. This structure or order generally has a coherence or consistency; although, inconsistencies may exist within one's worldview. This coherence, consistency, or order within one's worldview gives orientation and direction for living life. Therefore, a person must discover what is true and live a life compatible with that truth.

3. How do conflicting worldviews affect a culture? (71)

The collective worldviews of individuals generally form a society or nation, and one dominant worldview usually will exist and order society accordingly. As other groups with different or competing worldviews enter a society or nation, the resulting tensions and friction between the groups may lead to conflict. Wars are fought because of conflicting worldviews. Nations rise and fall because of worldviews. Freedoms are won or lost because of worldviews. Worldviews may shift or change from generation to generation, something that will be examined in this book. Such changes may lead to greater order or greater disorder.

4. Are all worldviews of equal value? (71-72)

16

The value of a worldview will be determined by whether or not the worldview's answers to life's most important questions are determined to be true. Some worldviews may contain elements of truth but will ultimately fail if enough leaven of false premises is mixed with the truth. Therefore, all worldviews are not equal because many contain only partial truths.

5. How does Princeton Professor Robert George define the conflict of worldviews in America? (72)

George states that the battle is not one between the world's major civilizations (the West, the Islamic world, and Confucian East) but a clash within the civilization of the West. This clash is between those holding the Judeo-Christian worldview and those who reject this worldview in favor of a humanist orthodoxy (of which feminism, multiculturalism, lifestyle liberalism, and gay liberationism are examples).

6. How do the humanists depict the combatants in the battle of worldviews? (72-73)

Humanists depict the battle as being between those persons of "faith" and those of "reason." They follow a dualistic worldview that limits the influence of faith to personal piety, efforts of the clergy, to the future kingdom, or a liberal social gospel. All other realms of human activity are considered humanist or worldly and within the province of reason and outside of religious or sacred influences. Areas excluded from divine influence include the family, politics, business, art, education, journalism, thought, emotion, plants and animals, and inanimate matter. However, the Christian believes that faith and reason are not in conflict within the Judeo-Christian worldview and that the real conflict is between faith allied with reason on the one hand and emotion and imagination on the other.

7. Why do humanists present secularism as a neutral doctrine that deserves privileged status as the national public philosophy and what is the Christian's response? (73)

Secularism is supposed to be a view independent of tradition and that represents an arena upon which various traditions (Judaism,

Christianity, Marxism, etc.) can compete for the allegiance of the people. However, as the Christian points out, secularism is just another player in the battle of worldviews. And, as stated above, the major combatants in the West are the secular humanists and those adhering to the Judeo-Christian worldview.

8. In the West, why have secularists' tactics been so successful in its battle with the Judeo-Christian worldview? (73)

With Americans exhibiting a pervasive ignorance of American history and tradition and with an almost universal assault by the government, media, and academia, the Judeo-Christian concepts of government, sexuality, human life, religion, and morality in public life have been battered.

Chapter 5 – The Fingerprints of God

1. How is it that a perceived truth that transcends the senses and time can be understood by both the ancient philosophers and modern primitives? (78)

The Apostle Paul answered this question in Romans 2:13-16 RSV. "For it is not the hearers of the law who are righteous before God, but the doers of the law who will be justified. When Gentiles who have not the law do by nature what the law requires, they are a law to themselves, even though they do not have the law. They show that what the law requires is *written on their hearts*, while their conscience also bears witness and their conflicting thoughts accuse or perhaps excuse them on that day when, according to my gospel, God judges the secrets of men by Christ Jesus."

2. Upon what must a worldview be conditioned? (78)

A worldview must be conditioned by wisdom and common sense and therefore is not a matter of education or intellectual brilliance. A worldview that lacks wisdom and common sense is not workable. A workable worldview is one that is coherent or consistent and gives orientation and direction for living life. Academic disciplines such as theology and philosophy are scientific and theoretical whereas worldview is a matter of the shared daily experiences of mankind. It is an inescapable component of all human knowing. Worldview belongs to an order of cognition more basic than that of science or theory.

3. What are those things thought to be mysterious and superior, and worthy of being sought to the exclusion of everything else? (78-79)

Those things are called norms, the permanent things, to which mankind must adhere in order to live. It is a moral order that transcends time. It is not instinct. It is not learned behavior through time although the recognition and practice of those norms are important to keep those norms visible and alive for following generations. The norms or permanent things are applicable to all of mankind and to all ages. In the revelation of the order of the universe to the Hebrews, it pointed back to the beginning of mankind when all men knew of good and evil. But as time advanced man's understanding of good and evil diminished. The revelation to the Hebrews and the first century Christians, recorded over a 1,600-year span of time, gave illumination, order, and meaning to those pre-revelation norms or permanent things and which mankind perceived and endeavored to know. Together, the norms or permanent things and the revelation of the order of the universe as created by God form an inescapable component of all human knowing.

4. Describe Russell Kirk's perceptions of the need for order in our lives and the consequences of a life lived without order. (79-80)

"Order is the path we follow, or the pattern by which we live with purpose and meaning. Above food and shelter…we must have order. The human condition is insufferable unless we perceive a harmony, an order in existence." Kirk identified two roots of order: the order of the soul (moral order) and the order of the republic (social order), and they are intricately linked and dependent on each other. Disorder of one leads to disorder of the other. The Supreme Being created the universe, and in His creation a certain order was implemented. This order is reflected in certain norms for living life and which are called by other names including universals, permanent things, eternal truths, and first principles. Actions that conflict with this Supreme Being's laws will bring disorder and distress to one's life. Much of the modern world remains ignorant of or rejects the revelation of who God is and His plan for man's redemption from his human condition. Thus, man lives in various states of confusion and disorder as he seeks solace through various false gods and ideologies only to find continued disorder. He recognizes and experiences disorder but has not the will or knowledge to find order.

5. What are Blackstone's twin pillars of the law and why are they important? (80-81)

When the Supreme Being formed the universe and created matter out of nothing, he impressed certain principles (laws) upon that matter, from which it can never depart, and without which it would cease to be. Blackstone's twin pillars of the law are the law of nature and the

20

law of revelation, and upon these all human laws must rest. These laws reveal certain truths that are intrinsic and timeless, and those truths are essential elements that provide a coherent and rational way to live in the world. Blackstone stated that the laws of human nature are so inseparably interwoven with the happiness of each individual that man's happiness cannot be obtained without observing and adhering to those laws. Only a worldview that aligns with those timeless truths will allow its adherents to live in a harmonious relationship with nature and those around them.

6. What is the difference between the laws of nature and laws of human nature? (82)

Unlike obedience to the laws of nature, man has a choice as to whether to obey or disobey the norms or laws of human nature. But as with the laws of nature, violation of the laws of human nature also has negative consequences. In regards to the laws of human nature, most societies deem certain actions to be bad (e.g., stealing, murder) and will impose consequences (penalties, imprisonment, or death) on those who violate its collective worldview. Other norms such as the nuclear family, fair play, and honesty are deemed to be good.

7. How does a society develop a collective worldview and with what must it align itself? (83-84)

A society develops a worldview as it adopts a system of moral codes and laws whereby it enforces what it believes is right and good for society. For that society to survive, that worldview must align with those hidden but largely discernible rules that produce specific, predictable outcomes to orient or bring order to a society, that is, to make a civil society civil. When a society ignores or abandons those discernible rules that bring order to a society, one begins to see the tatters as the cohesive fabric of that society begins to unravel and shred.

8. What are the questions that every worldview or belief system must answer? (84)

What is the nature and structure of our world and how does it function? Where are we heading? What shall we do (values)? How should we attain our goals? What is true and false? Colson and Pearcey have reduced these to three universal questions: Where did we come from, and who are we? What has gone wrong with the world? What can we do to fix it?" Answers to these questions allow one to evaluate any area of life (e.g., family life, politics, science, education, the arts, and popular culture) and how each area aligns with one's worldview.

9. Define the following terms and their relative positions in American life: modernism, post-Christian and postmodernism. (84-85)

Modernists are little concerned about social issues and ideology and tend to be leaders in business, government, science, and the military. Technology and material success were their most important goals. Modernism dominated American culture for most of the twentieth century. But as the century progressed, America began sliding into both the post-modern and post-Christian era. By post-Christian is meant that Judeo-Christian truths are no longer the basis of American and other Western cultures as it relates to public philosophy and moral consensus. One step beyond is postmodernism. Postmodernists hold that there are no universal truths and believe all social constructions are shaped by class, gender, and ethnicity in which all viewpoints, lifestyles, and beliefs are equally valid.

10. What is the Christian worldview? (86)

God existed before the universe was created, and then God created the universe and all that is within it including the laws that govern that creation. Unlike all of the other elements of his creation, man was created with a free will. This part of the Christian worldview is called Creation. Mankind's free will allowed man to think and act in ways that were contrary to God's plan and will for His creation. When man acted in ways contrary to God's laws (truths), such disobedience to God's laws was called sin, and as a result decay and death entered into God's creation. This is called the Fall, and it affected not only man but all of God's creation. But as God is a loving God, he created a way through His son, Jesus Christ, which allows man to bring order to the chaos he created. This is called the Restoration. There you have the basic elements of the Christian worldview: the Creation, the Fall, and the Restoration.

Chapter 6 – The Judeo-Christian Tradition and the Rise of Western Civilization

1. What became of Christianity at the fall of the Roman Empire in the fifth century? (88)

With the decline and fall of the western half of the Roman Empire by the end of the fifth century, the material and cultural center of Christianity moved to Constantinople, the heir of Greece and Rome. Yet, a remnant of the Christian heritage of the western portion of the Roman Empire was pushed northward into the sparse and hostile forests of France and western Germany. The inhabitants were Gauls whom the Romans had conquered and brought civilization at the beginning of the Christian era. To this group was added a smaller number of Teutonic invaders that had come from the east and hindered for a time the building of an organized social life and assimilation of the Mediterranean culture.

2. Under what conditions did the remnant of Christianity live after they fled to Europe from the failed Roman Empire, and how did their society develop? (88)

Life was harsh in the pioneer wilds of northern Europe at the beginning of the Middle Ages around A.D. 500. It was also the beginning of what was called the Dark Ages, a time when life was focused on the physical demands of survival and less on those tasks required of a cultivated society. Compared to the remainder of the civilized world, these simple agricultural people of France and Germany would appear backwards if not uncivilized. Yet, out of such stock grew Western civilization, and by Western civilization is meant Christendom. Because the Western peoples began with so little and struggled under harsh conditions, the Dark Ages would not end until the eleventh century. However, from about 1100 to 1300, the men of Western Europe built a cohesive and somewhat refined civilization, and the broad and general characteristics of their medieval society remained for centuries. Those characteristics and viewpoints, i.e., worldview, became the ideas and ideals that are the foundations of modern Christendom.

3. What happened to the eastern half of the Christian world following its fall to the Turks and what was the impact on Western civilization? (89)

The Middle Ages that began a thousand years before with the fall of Rome in 476 ended in 1453 when Constantinople fell to the Turks. The Byzantine scholars and nobles fled to Italy and brought a new "humanism" centered on ancient Greek civilization, an essentially pagan view of human nature, concerned with the present as opposed to the focus of the medieval church and institutions on other-worldliness. The ancient Greeks considered man to be the center of existence. Reason, not emotion, was the true fountain of knowledge, and the emphasis on reason to attain the improvement of humanity is called humanism.

4. What is Christian humanism and what was its effect on the Age of Faith? (89)

Following the arrival of the Byzantine scholars and nobles in Italy, the Europeans began a renewed interest in the culture of ancient Greece's classical civilization, the essence of which was the new humanism that focused on the "dignity of man" or man regenerate. This was the beginning of Christian humanism—not a dethronement of God but the belief that through the moral disciplines of humanistic learning one struggles toward God. But as Kirk wrote, "...the seed of intellectual arrogance, overweening self-confidence, was sown. A time would come when man would take himself for the be-all and end-all." The heresies of the immigrants from the fallen Byzantine Empire accelerated the Renaissance and hastened the end of the Age of Faith.

5. How did two thirteenth century Christian philosophers profoundly affect the course of Christianity and the Catholic Church and who were they? (89-90)

Albert the Great and his pupil, Thomas Aquinas, were the first within the church to support the teachings of Aristotle. The teachings of these men along with the coming of the universities sowed the seeds for the destruction of the medieval focus on realism—the existence of universals—by clearing the path for the Renaissance and later the Age of Enlightenment.

6. What is the nominalist doctrine and how did it further undermine the focus on realism in the fourteenth century? (90)

William of Ockham and his nominalist doctrine denied the existence of universals through the separation of philosophy from theology.

7. Following the centralization of the power of the church under the papacy during the twelfth and thirteenth centuries, certain abuses occurred within the church which lasted to the beginning of the sixteenth century and coincided with the Renaissance and later Age of Enlightenment. What were these occurrences and events that would forever change the church? (90-91)

The Roman church's penitential system had deteriorated to such a point that forgiveness became a matter of gifts of money. As a Catholic priest, Martin Luther had striven to attain righteousness as the Apostle Paul had done through endless confessions and ascetic practices. In this desperate spiritual quest he experienced a "conversion" in which he saw the truth of justification by faith only through the grace of God as opposed to works. The Reformation is recognized as having begun in July 1517 when Luther nailed his ninety-five theses to the door of the church in Wittenberg, Germany. The Reformation was not a challenge to the universals but a call to reform within the Church and a return to the fundamental principles of the gospel of Jesus Christ. Thus, the Reformation was the product of the abhorrence of decadence within the Church and the Church's flirtation with the new doctrines and enticements of the Renaissance. From these twin afflictions arose Luther and his doctrine of the priesthood of all believers which shook the foundations of the Christian church and ultimately led to the establishment of the Protestantism.

8. What was the result of the schism between the two great arms of the Church? (91-92)

The schism resulted in a religious war. While each of the two great arms of the Church were at the other's throat, the artistic, intellectual, and social movement of the Renaissance would challenge the Christian faith with a denial of the understanding of the fallen nature of man (the human condition), denial of Christian teachings, and a glorification of the pleasures of the flesh. Thus, the European Enlightenment may be said to be the child of the European Renaissance and the religious wars following the Reformation. (91-92)

9. What was the Enlightenment, when did it occur, and what was its center? (92)

The closing years of the 1600s and all of the 1700s are considered to be the period of Enlightenment in which mathematical philosophies and scientific discoveries were applied to moral and social concerns. The Age of Enlightenment was a period of a particularly strong intellectual propensity with regard to the doctrines of progress, rationality, secularism, and political reform. The articulation of the new social order was made by the Enlightenment philosophers of the era, particularly those of France. The capstone of Enlightenment thought lay in the *Encyclopedia,* the twenty-one volume repository of knowledge and propaganda of the French philosophers with publication beginning in1751-1752.

10. Through the Enlightenment came the notion that there were no moral values that arose from fixed ideas of right and wrong. Describe this concept and its consequences. (93)

To Enlightenment philosophers, moral values were the product of the mind as one experienced pleasure and pain and consequently did not arise from fixed ideas of right and wrong. The enormous consequences of this concept on civilization were incalculable and have had a dominating influence on theories about education, economics, and other disciplines.

Chapter 7 – The Renaissance and Enlightenment – Progress and Perfection – Science and Reason

1. While the Catholics and Protestants were at war, the champions of the Renaissance and Enlightenment used two weapons in their attack on faith. What were these weapons? (95)

Science and reason were used as a wedge to split asunder the foundation upon which faith rested.

2. How did Enlightenment philosophers use science to challenge the Christianity? (95)

Science was the first tool in the hands of Enlightenment philosophers to be used to achieve the ideal society through the manipulation of nature. The new science sought power over nature for the service of man and in the process broke with the Middle Ages in an understanding of the cosmos, planet earth, and now physical man. The new science exploded in the nineteenth century and would challenge one of the basic underpinnings of Christianity—faith in the Creator who created man in His own image. (95)

3. How do humanists view Christianity and Enlightenment thought? (97)

Humanists believe there *is* a war between Christianity and Enlightenment thought. One must be true and the other false—they cannot co-exist. Humanists use science to challenge Christianity, universal truths, and the revelation of those truths.

4. The author gives three reasons for the success of humanists in promoting this perceived conflict between science and Christianity. What is the first reason? (97)

The average man accepts this view because the popular media, scientific journals, and textbooks continue to promote the myth of a conflict between science and Christianity, that science has won the battle, and that the ascendancy of science beginning in the seventeen century caused of the demise of religion.

5. How do Christians view religion and science? (97)

The Christian sees no conflict with science when he or she believes that God created the universe and put the universal truths in place. As Colson wrote, "…it was Christianity that made science possible…the scientific method, and all it has accomplished, [and] is a great apologetic argument for the truth of Christianity."

6. What was the humanist objective in creating a conflict between science and religion? (97-98)

The conflict between science and religion escalated at the end of the nineteenth century through the efforts of scientists and educational leaders in order to wrest control of their institutions from the Church, a strategy to achieve cultural power. The division between science and religion was manufactured and not an intellectual separation.

7. A second reason that humanists have succeeded in creating the perceived conflict between science and religion is the belief that science has disproved Christianity and thereby reinforces the supposed gap between scientific truth and the Christian myth. What is the Christian's answer to this assertion? (98-99)

When conducting a scientific investigation, scientists must still deal only with things that can be known and measured. Consequently, scientific naturalism concludes, incorrectly, that if science can't test for supernatural causes, then the supernatural cannot exist. Timothy Keller wrote, "It is one thing to say that science is only equipped to test for natural causes and cannot speak to any others. It is quite another to insist that science proves that no other causes could possibly exist."

8. The author speaks of three ways of knowing or defining reality. Humanists accept two but Christians put forward a third. Explain the three ways of determining or knowing reality. (99-100)

The first is knowing reality through the senses. A second rests in the noumenal realm in which something that is unknowable by the senses is conceivable by reason. Christians see a third level of reality—a *knowing* that transcends both the senses (physical and material) and understanding (reason). Here we enter into a realm akin to faith for faith is a belief, a knowing. Such knowing or faith does not rest upon but *transcends* the senses, desires, emotions, measurement, scientists' feeble attempts at proof, and even reason itself. Through faith we enter into the reality of the supernatural.

9. What is a third reason humanists have succeeded in creating the perceived conflict between science and Christianity? (101-102)

Humanists have successfully diverted attention from their own failures and inconsistencies. This diversion is accomplished through both substitution and attack. Substitution occurs when humanistic scientific theories and dicta (that contradict or challenge the truth of Christianity and its doctrines) are found to be false. They quickly replace the false suppositions with new theories that continue to support their humanistic worldview. The mistakes are merely viewed as steps on a path to new knowledge in man's ever-progressing march towards perfection. Diversion of attention from the failures of scientific tenets of humanism is also achieved through attacking those who question or criticize those failures, falsities, and inconsistencies as being neurotic, ignorant, bigoted, or whatever appears to be the most effective. Therefore, exceptional hostility and vitriol are directed toward those of a Christian worldview by institutions that have vested interests in the humanistic worldview (media, education, government, science, sociology, and the arts).

10. The first weapon used by humanists in attacking faith was science. What is the second weapon and how did it arise? (103-104)

The second weapon is reason or the intellect. Naturalism imagines that scientific laws are adequate to account for all phenomena and denies the supernatural. Naturalism also contends that action, desires, or thought is based only on natural desires and instincts. If nature is all there is, then rational thought (reason and understanding) must have come into existence through an evolutionary process and the consequent gradual disappearance of those less fitted to survive. In other words, the naturalist contends that natural selection, which must preserve and increase useful behavior, somehow turns sub-rational thought into rational, inferential thinking that reaches truth.

11. What is the Christian view of reason? (105)

For Christianity, Divine reason is older than nature, and from Divine reason comes nature in all of its orderliness. Because of this orderliness of nature, mankind may know her. Man was created with the ability to reason, and that ability is not part of the system of nature but something apart. Man's reason is not a "thing" but an ability to comprehend, infer, and think—something we do. When man reasons, his reasoning may be faulty or he may have correct or right reasoning.

12. How does God help man when man has faulty reasoning? (105)

First, man was created in his image, and thus there is something of God's nature in us—something of a homing instinct for the Divine. Second, God gave us road signs in the form of universals that serve as guides to our reasoning. Lastly, He gave us revelation through the books written by the inspired Hebrews and first century Christians. By these standards, all of life should be measured and right reason obtained.

13. The author states that reason is an ally of faith. What does he mean? (106)

Our reasoning leads us to belief, that is, belief in the truth of Christianity and all upon which it rests. That belief has been derived from our observation and reasoning abilities. That belief has been tested and found to be truth. In the sense used here, faith "…is the art of holding on to things your reason has once accepted, in spite of your changing moods." In time faith grows to be more important to our belief in the truth than our reasoning ability. Through faith, we can withstand changes in our moods, our failures, our doubts, our circumstances, or any other of life's challenges.

14. How do the Catholic and Protestant views of reason differ? (107-110)

The Roman Catholic philosophy is based on Aristotle who posited that the objective moral order was knowable by human reason and obtainable through free will. In other words, a well-ordered soul has rule over emotion. The evangelical Protestant's understanding of reason differs with regard to the route to free choice, and that route is "…being born again through Christ. Reason by itself, diseased as it is, will not get us there." Without being born again, we cannot successfully guide our lives because of our impaired or flawed reason. To sum up, the Catholic believes that free will can be ruled and reined in by reason. The Protestant says the battle between reason and emotion was won at Calvary through the blood of Jesus and the Cross. When one is born again, he is in Christ, and he died, was buried, and was resurrected with Him and is no longer slave to sin as he abides in Christ.

15. If man's reason is faulty due to man's corrupted nature, of what value is reason to the Christian? (111)

As faulty as reason may be in fallen man, reason is not banished by Blackstone or the evangelical Protestant. In one sense reason takes us to the door of Christianity, but faith invites us in and holds our hand as we continue the faith journey. However, reason was not left at the door. As we move along the faith journey, we encounter life— all sorts of thoughts, ideas, things, situations, difficulties, trials, struggles, disappointments, opportunities, and so forth. Thus, Christians must examine life and through reason filter it through his or her worldview.

Chapter 8 – Colonial American Heritage

1. What were the two pillars upon which the Founders created the American Government? (115)

One was the moral pillar of the Judeo-Christian tradition and the other was the political pillar of English history and law with elements from the ancient Greeks and Romans.

2. What was the source of the American heritage of liberty? (115-116)

The origins of liberty were medieval and not of the Renaissance or Enlightenment. The colonists brought with them the British system of law which relied on tradition rather than theoretical schemes of abstract reason. The central focus of this tradition was the common law that had existed from "time immemorial." It was during the Middle Ages that the foundations of free government were established as opposed to the ideas of ancient Greek and Roman cultures.

3. How did the concepts of a free government through constitutionalism arise during the Middle Ages? (116-117)

The concept of a free government and constitutionalism arose through the efforts of the Catholic Church that consistently challenged the kings of the Middle Ages and the decentralized nature of the powers and military forces that arose under the feudal barons. From these two sources came the English freedoms such as the growth of Parliament, safeguards for property, legal privilege, taxation by consent, and other concessions and guarantees that were expressed through the English common law tradition. And without question the source of these freedoms that became the bedrock of the American system of government was medieval Christendom.

4. How were the traditions of English law and constitutionalism that had grown over a thousand years challenged in Britain between the beginning of the Reformation in 1517 and the Glorious Revolution of 1688? (117)

There was almost continual conflict between the English kings and Parliament that would severely test the medieval advances toward freedom. It was the English kings' reliance on pagan doctrines of the Renaissance that promoted Roman legal theories of the absolutist nature of royal power. Parliament was weakened by disunity and conflicts among the various elements of the feudal power bases, the development of a court party within the Parliament, and other changes that weakened the system of restraints on royal power. The most damaging challenge to English law and constitutionalism came during the reign of Henry VIII when he broke with the Catholic Church and vastly increased his power and wealth through confiscation of the property of the Church and replacement of the vigilant priests with clerics of compromise that supported Henry's church.

5. What effect did the English kings' challenges to the traditions of English law and constitutionalism have on those fleeing England for the American colonies? (118)

The defense of English law and constitutionalism against the designs of the absolutist kings of England was indelibly imprinted on the minds of the American immigrants of the early 1600s. This understanding was retained and greatly influenced the Founders in their design of the new American government 150 years later.

6. What was the primary reason the colonists came to America? (118)

Colonists wanted religious liberty. And upon this fundamental desire, substantially all of the thirteen colonies were founded.

7. What is deism and to why did it not greatly influence the American colonies during the eighteen century? (120-121)

To deists of the era, the Supreme Being was the creator of the universe but uninvolved in its operation and direction. For deists, Jesus was a great moral teacher but not the redeemer. Nature and rationalism were man's guides, not revelation. Deism contradicted Christianity by declaring man was intrinsically good and must be liberated from superstition, fear, and belief in the corrupt nature of man. However, the Americans were a practical people and often skeptical of abstract concepts such as the perfectibility of man and society; the dismissal of religion as mere superstition; over-reliance on reason; and speedy intellectual, political, and social change. Therefore, Enlightenment thought including deism did not greatly penetrate the colonies.

8. The author describes three reasons that illustrate the relatively inconsequential influence of deism and Enlightenment thought in the eighteenth century as a foundation for the Revolution and founding of the United States. Name and briefly describe each of those reasons. (123-126)

The first reason was the experiences of the colonists since their arrival in America. The practical Americans knew the realities of life in the wilderness were far removed from the intellectual speculations and theories of the Renaissance and Enlightenment built upon the myths and failures of societies and institutions long gone. They resorted to their faith that had sustained them through the hardship and deprivations in the wilderness and built a society based on English traditions, customs, laws, and patrimony that emerged from the Middle Ages. (123)

The second reason was the spiritual renewal known as the Great Awakening and the revivals that flowed from its beginning in the 1840s. From these revivals sprang rapid growth of many new and popular churches, the movement for popular education, a new emphasis on political democracy, and in the end substantially enhanced the attitudes and efforts of the colonists as they sought independence from a dictatorial and capricious English crown and Parliament during the last third of the century. (123-125)

A third force that stemmed the tide of Enlightenment thinking was that the Founders' realization that freedom would not be possible under the onerous English laws and limitations placed on them. The crown and Parliament began exerting new controls on the heretofore brash and independent-minded Americans. The changes involved the basic freedoms in religion, politics, and commerce that colonists had come to enjoy. Radical changes by the mother country were now being imposed in direct contravention to British law and traditionalism built up over the centuries. (125-126)

Chapter 9 – The American Founders and Their Beliefs

1. Although the American colonies did not exhibit a significant hierarchy of classes as was present in England, the author discusses several broad groups that comprised American colonial society. Identify these groups and movements between groups. (129-130)

The broad upper group was comprised of working capitalists, merchants, entrepreneurs, planters, and land speculators. A large middle group was comprised of ordinary freeholding farmers, small planters, some tenant farmers, master artisans, and shopkeepers. The bottom ranks of colonial society included poor, landless individuals; freed servants that had completed their period of indenture; squatters and poor whites; the unfortunate, old, indigent, debilitated, and insane. Indentured servants and slaves did not form a single laboring class that was an institutional component of colonial society. Rather, they were an appendage to colonial society, and served as a discomfiting supplement to the pool of laborers; although, the slave population played a significant role in the economics of the southern colonies. Unlike the uncrossable lines found in England and Europe, the composition of the various groups exhibited a certain fluidity that made possible movement from one group to another by hard work and a bit of luck.

2. Why did both early and modern historians discount the role of religion in the Revolutionary period, and why is their view not supported by the historical record? (131-132)

The fact that political and wartime concerns took precedence over publications of a religious nature gave the misleading impression of a decline of religious interest and fervor. Also, an appearance of religious decline resulted from a significant decrease in the percentage of state-oriented churches (Anglican, Congregational, and Presbyterian) between 1860 and 1890, but this decline was more than offset by growth of new denominations such as the Baptists, Methodists, and others. During the 30 year period the combined growth of the Methodists and Baptists rose from 94 congregations in 1760 to over 1,500 in 1790.

3. What were the religious beliefs of Americans during the
    Revolutionary period and how did these beliefs impact the
    design of American government? (132)

The Founders believed that the fingerprints of God were etched on the
heart of man from the moment of his creation and that man is happiest
when he functions in accord with God's grand design for man, the
world, and the laws of the universe. Because of the manner of his
creation, man has had the ability, the freedom to walk a path of
independence from God and God's laws. The freedom to test those
limits, to step outside of the boundaries, is within the nature of man.
Therefore, the nature of man was corruptible, and the design of
government must account for this human condition.

4. What were the fundamental differences between the French
    and American Revolutions as described by Edmund Burke and
    others? (133)

The French revolutionaries, hoping to transform utterly human society
and even human nature, broke with the past, defied history, embraced
theoretic dogmas, and so fell under the domination of man-created
ideologies. The American Revolution was not so much a revolution
but a defense of their existing order against external interference and
the preservation of the institutions of representative government and
private rights that were based on English traditions and chartered
rights. The American colonials were merely asserting the rights of
Englishmen arising from old charters—creating a political separation
from England and not a social revolution.

5. In drafting the Constitution, the Founders examined the two
    extremes of the continuum of political power and control.
    What were these extremes, and how did the Founders design
    the Constitution to avoid these extremes? (134)

Anarchy on the one end provided no law, no government, and no
systematic control. Tyranny on the other end imposed too much
government, too much control, and too much oppression. Under the
one system there was no law; under the other was ruler's law. The
Founders chose a people's law that would reside at the center of the

continuum between anarchy and ruler's law. People's law would provide enough government to maintain security, justice, and good order, but not enough government to abuse the people.

6. What was the central difficulty the Founders recognized in drafting the Constitution to reflect the people's law? (134-135)

The Founders recognized they were constructing a framework for a government that must address the reality of human nature, a nature that was fundamentally corrupt and had remained unchanged through the ages. Therefore, the Constitution could not be custom built for one age or economy but had to stand the tests of time and to address unchanging human nature.

7. Explain what Constitutional liberals mean when they say the Constitution should be a "living document", and what are the dangers thereof? (136-137)

By living document, the Constitutional liberals believe that its meaning and intent should be an instrument for enlightened social change which would allow it to be modified or bent to address the modern age and problems never foreseen by the Founders. Therefore, human nature, through its passions, appetites, and desires of the moment, is released from the prescriptions of history, custom, convention, and tradition. This was not the intent of the Founders. The danger is that thoughtful interpretation of the law is thrown aside in favor of passion and expediency that are employed to make law. The efforts of the modern liberal-progressive to imbue (read into or interpret) the Constitution with new rights and doctrines to meet or address the changes of a modern world travel the same slippery path as those of the French Revolution who based their changes on some ethereal, imaginary, or invented "rights of man" that attempted to address the failings of human nature.

Chapter 10 – The Roots and Rise of Modern Humanism

1. What civilization and in what period did the man-made philosophy of humanism receive significant advancement? (139)

The Greeks of the fourth through sixth centuries BC gave form and body to the man-made philosophy of humanism that would impact the world second only to Jesus Christ.

2. How does J. M. Roberts describe the influence of the Greeks with regard to humanism? (140)

Roberts called the Greek poets' and philosophers' challenge to irrationality (belief in the supernatural) in social and intellectual activity the greatest single achievement that has flowed from that pre-eminent civilization. In other words, the Greeks believed that an explanation of things apart from God could be found; that the world did not ultimately rest upon the meaningless and arbitrary fiat of gods or demons.

3. What were the fundamental beliefs of Plato which stood in opposition to the humanistic Greek philosophers of the age? (141)

Plato believed in the immortality of the soul, the existence of divine moral laws, that the soul should be cleansed from false desires and appetites that degrade the soul so that we may conform to the divine law, and that the soul is separate from the body and eternal.

4. Describe the first clash between the humanistic worldview of the Greeks and that of infant Christianity in the first century AD. (145)

The Apostle Paul preached to the gathered Athenians at Mars' Hill. Paul presented the Creator and then challenged their idolatry and rejected the notions that God could be presented as an image, dwelled in temples made with hands, or was "...worshipped with men's hands, as though he needed anything." Lastly, Paul calls the Athenians to repentance for their idolatry. Although Paul's preaching was brilliant, only a few believed.

5. What did Thomas Aquinas believe with regard to the classical and Christian explanations of the world and what were the consequences? (148)

Aquinas believed that the classical world of the Greeks was the forerunner of the Christian era, and in his *Summa Theologica* he attempted to reconcile the two explanations of the world. With Christendom's embrace of the classical came a revival of humanistic letters in the fourteenth through sixteenth centuries and opened the door for the humanistic opposition to Christianity during the Renaissance and Age of Enlightenment.

6. In *The Philosophy of Humanism,* written in 1949, Dr. Corliss Lamont lists ten central propositions to describe the humanist philosophy. Summarize each. (149-150)

*   All forms of the supernatural are myths and that Nature is the totality of being and exists independently of any mind or consciousness.
*   Man is the evolutionary product of Nature, and his mind is inextricably joined with the functioning of his brain. Therefore, there is no conscious survival after death due to the unity of body and personality.
*   Through reason and the scientific method, man can solve his own problems.
*   Humans are masters of their own destiny and have freedom of choice and action.
*   Human values are grounded in this-earthy experiences and relationships. Happiness, freedom, and progress *in this world* are the highest goals of all mankind.
*   Life is harmonious when personal satisfactions and continuous self-development are joined with work and activities that support community welfare.
*   Extensive development of art and an awareness of beauty promote an esthetic experience that can become a pervasive reality in the lives of men.

- Extensive social programs are necessary for the establishment of democracy, peace, a high standard of living, and a thriving economic order.
- Freedom of expression and civil liberties in all areas of life through democratic procedures and parliamentary governments come from the complete social implementation of reason and the scientific method.
- Humanism rests on the unending questioning of basic assumptions and convictions including those assumptions and convictions upon which humanism itself rests. (149-150)

7. Briefly summarize the elements of the two basic branches of humanism as described by Lamont. (150-151)

Naturalism considers that human beings, the earth, and the unending universe of space and time are all parts of one great Nature. The whole of existence is equivalent to Nature and outside of Nature noting exists. Naturalism has no place for a supernatural God. Materialism is a close cousin of Naturalism but tends to lump the behavior of living creatures and human beings to the operation of the same laws that apply to inanimate existence.

Chapter 11 – The "Why"—Worldviews of Humanism and Christianity

1. The author states that there are three ways in which man can obtain clues as to why God created the universe and mankind. What are these three ways? (157)

Reading the biblical revelation of truth, examination of those universal truths evident in various societies throughout history, and by looking at man as we were created in His image and therefore we can see elements that reflect God and His character.

2. How is man's need for relationships a reflection of the character of God? (157-158)

The importance of human relationships is a reflection of the Trinitarian relationship, a picture of His fundamental being. God's being is shown by the Father-Son relationship and the relationship of Christ with the Church of which He is the head and we are the body. For mankind, the relational pattern is present in various entities—marriage, family, community, nations, and the Kingdom of God.

3. In describing man's chief end as glorifying God by communing with God forever, the author discusses the reason God gave man a free will. Discuss that reason. (158)

God did not create man out of need. Rather, it was a will to love, an expression of the very character of God, to share the inner life of the Trinity. In other words, God chose to love man. God also allowed man the choice of loving Him by giving man a free will. But creating man with a free will meant the possibility of rejection of God and His love. In other words free will and the potential for rejection of God was the penalty for the possibility of love.

4. What was the penalty for rejection of God? (158)

Man's rejection of God created a broken relationship and thus separated himself and his family from God. Although God's love and plan for mankind never wavered, yet the gulf separating man from God was un-crossable. For man, the emptiness caused by his broken relationship and separation from his creator tormented his soul. Man desperately sought to restore to that relationship, but he knew not how. Faint hints from the past stirred vague memories imprinted in his being. Those hints were the permanent things, universal truths that pointed to the laws which guided the universe, nature, and human nature.

5. What are the permanent things, universal truths that point to the laws which guide the universe, nature, and human nature and what is their connection to the biblical revelation? (159)

These universal truths are found in many cultures and are not confined to the Judeo-Christian writings. Examples of these universal truths include special duties to parents and elders, special duties to my wife and child, duties of good faith and veracity, duties to the weak, the poor and the desolate. These norms provide a common human law of action which can over-arch rulers and ruled alike. The revelation to the Hebrews brought clarity, definition, and focus to those truths by which man must live. More importantly, the revelation pointed to the Savior who would act as that bridge to span the gulf between man and God. Jesus Christ is God's son and became the advocate for man and a means of man's redemption from his sin.

6. When humanists attempt to discredit Christianity and belief in an omnipotent, benevolent, and personal God by saying that the immensity of the universe could only be known to modern man, how does the Christian respond? (161)

The tens of thousands of stars visible to the ancients had as much impact on their understanding of the immensity of space as the impact on the modern astronomer when peering into the vast reaches of space with the most powerful telescope. Contrary to humanists' assertions, modern science has not radically altered the primitive picture of things that encourage the Christian religious view. The vastness of space, whether seen or unseen, is neither a modern concept nor a legitimate argument against Christianity.

7. How does the humanist view the age of the universe? (161)

Many humanists believe the universe is eternal as opposed to having a beginning initiated by a Creator or First Mover. Humanists claim that creative matter, the stuff of the universe, does not need a Prime Mover to jump start the universe and keep it going. On the contrary, it is claimed that the universe is auto-dynamic in its existence, operation, development, and continuation. Given its age and dynamic nature, many humanists call the universe an eternally existing reality and assert that it is not logically necessary to accept the conclusion that there is a beginning in time and, by extension, a supernatural God as Creator or First Cause.

8. Humanists point to the enormous time spans and eternally existing nature of the cosmos as evidence that speaks against Christianity. How does the Christian respond? (161-162)

The Christian contends that there was a beginning to time, and science seems to confirm that contention. Stephen Hawking states that before 1915 space and time were thought of as being fixed, i.e., that space and time continued forever. However, Hawking and his associate, Roger Penrose, showed that Einstein's general theory of relativity implied that the universe must have a beginning and, perhaps, an end.

9. With regard to the creation of the universe, what is the scientific evidence that points to the existence of God and the purposeful design of the world for man? (163-164)

The conditions necessary for the development of intelligent life on earth are present in very limited areas throughout the universe. The necessary conditions are dictated by fifteen constants. These constants appear to have been very precisely adjusted to make possible the universe as we see it. These constants (e.g., gravitational constant, strong and weak nuclear force) have precise values. Francis Collins states that , "If any one of those constants was off by even one part in a million, or in some cases, by one part in a million million, the universe could not have actually come to the point where we see it. Matter would not have been able to coalesce; there would have been no galaxy, stars, planets, or people. Stephen Hawking has said, "The odds against a universe like ours emerging out of something like the Big Bang are enormous. I think there are clearly religious implications...It would be very difficult to explain why the universe would have begun in just this way except as the act of a God who intended to create beings like us."

10. With regard to the connection between the mind and physical body, the humanists hold to the monistic theory while Christians hold to the dualistic theory. Describe the two theories. (166)

Humanists hold to the monistic theory which sees such a close and fundamental connection of body and personality (including all aspects of the mind) and results in an indissoluble unity. Implicit in this theory is that the personality is not immortal and that man's earthly existence is all there is. Christians and certain other religions adhere to a dualistic view that the soul (will, intellect, emotions) is separate and independent from the body and that the soul survives the body's death. From this seminal difference flow enormous consequences for man in the areas of knowledge, ethics, education, and individual freedom.

Part III – Worldview

1. What was the secular revolution that began about 1870 as described by Christian Smith? (169)

The secular revolution represented a displacement of the dominant Protestant power and authority and secularism's capture and transformation of culture and institutions that govern the nation's public life.

2. What was the consequence of the secular revolution? (169)

The secularization process resulted in the separation of "…historic religious organization and authority from public institutions and relegating them to private life."

Chapter 12 – Religion – The Power of Religion in American History

1. Richard Weaver called man a special creature with two selves. What did he mean?
(171-172)

The first self is man's animal being, "…an organism living in an environment." What makes man different or special is the second half of his being. This second half involves man's understanding of the picture of himself that is derived from his spirit. This image or picture is the subjective part of man's being and is comprised of his wishes, hopes, imaginations, and desire to see things beyond himself. In effect, man must fit this picture of himself into a relationship with all other things. There is an urge to bring this image into focus and harmony with the surrounding world.

2. How does the author describe religion and the power thereof?
(172-173)

Men cannot detach themselves from religious beliefs. Religion is endemic to all of mankind, in every age and every people group. The power of religion results because man is a created being, his soul seeks the afterlife, and he searches for and relies on those permanent things that recur in every period of history. The power of religion grows because it is not linked to human experiment, invention, or ideologies but to the permanent things or first principles.

3. What is the humanists' view of religion and its origin? (173)

In the humanist world man is not to be directed by religion. For the humanist, religion is an entirely human social construction whose function is merely to draw people to gather and give meaning to their lives. There is no room for any worldview in which supernaturalism is a part. Religion is merely a form of human experience and values, and such experience and values are empty and meaningless if it "…substitutes a dead God for a living ideal of human justice." Humanists deny the dualism that divides the universe into two separate realms—the material and the spiritual.

4. Are all religions of equal value or worth? (174)

Man must seek answers to life's basic questions, and religion is the means whereby he seeks those answers. But many religions give false or inadequate pictures of life and thus fail to give man satisfaction in his quest for answers. Through these religions man's picture of himself becomes distorted and out of focus which results in a disorder of the soul as the questions of life remain unanswered. A religion must point to eternal truths if it is to adequately answer the basic questions of life.

5. What weapons do humanists use to undermine Christianity and what is the Christian's response? (174)

Humanists use science and reason in their efforts to undermine Christianity. However, Christianity does not surrender those weapons to the humanists. Properly understood, reason and science support the Judeo-Christian ethic. Ultimately, however, the battle is not to be won with reason and science but reliance on God's Word as recorded in the Bible.

6. How do humanists attempt to prove the falsity of the Bible and how should the Christian respond? (175-176)

A favorite tactic of humanists is to portray a war between science and religion. Humanists attempt to pull the Bible into the arena of science and scientific investigation to prove its falsity. We must remember that the Bible is not a science book, but it is also not anti-science. But Christian theologians have fallen into the humanist trap when they commit themselves enthusiastically to the detailed ideas of particular systems of scientific theory. Science has provided a great understanding of the natural world. However, the non-material things that are just as real in our human experience lie outside the capabilities of science to decipher. Such things include justice, love, fairness, morality, righteousness, charity, and mercy.

7. What was the purpose of the biblical revelation and in what manner was it presented? (176)

Fallen man needed a way to cross the gulf that separated him from God. Through the biblical revelation God pointed to a savior whose death, burial, and resurrection made possible the reunification of man with God. God revealed His message in words that would be intelligible for that people in that particular era. God's message had to be true and consistent with the nature of God and those universal truths that man sought and dimly perceived through the ages. Through history, poetry, prophecy, parable, and allegory, God painted the biblical mural or word picture of man's true story from his creation to his eternal destiny.

8. Define "inerrant" and "literal" as applied to the Bible. How do humanists use these terms to in their attempts to discredit the Bible, and what is the Christian response? (177)

"Inerrant" means without error. The meaning of "literal" implies a concern mainly with facts, and for the humanist that means facts that can be scientifically validated. But as has been stated, the Bible is a book of history, poetry, prophecy, parable, and allegory. All are part of the biblical revelation God used to paint an inerrant word picture of God and man and their relationship. Humanists attempt to force the inerrancy of the Bible into a laboratory test tube, but as previously stated the Bible deals with the non-material things that are outside the capabilities of science to decipher and are just as real in our human experience as any scientifically proven hypothesis.

9. If the infallibility of the Bible is derived from the belief that the words of the Scripture are God breathed (written by human hands but under the inspiration of God), how does the Christian defend the Bible's infallibility when the humanists attempt to undermine the authority of the Scripture by pointing to the numerous translations of the Bible through the centuries, and therefore claim the Bible can't be accurate as that of the original versions? (180)

The people of God of every age have pointed to the inerrancy of the Scripture, so too do they point to God's "providential preservation of the Scriptures." If we believe God gave great care to reveal his will and intent by causing inspired or God-breathed Scripture to be given to mankind, it is also reasonable to believe that God would not allow his Word to be corrupted. The Christian can rely on God's providential care in sustaining the accuracy of his revelation through the centuries and can confidently use standard and long accepted translations such as the Vulgate and King James versions as well as faithful modern translations.

Chapter 13 – Religion in the Public Arena – Mention Jesus Christ and "...all hell breaks loose"

1. How does the Christian respond when someone says that religion is such a deeply personal issue it is wrong to discuss what another person should believe? (182)

Our first response is to Christians. Christians that are faithful to Christ and his direction for living in this world must recognize the importance of sharing the Christian faith according to Matthew 28:19-20. For the secularist and humanist, we counter with two questions, "Why not discuss with someone what they should believe, either publicly or privately?" Who made the rule that we shouldn't? Some will counter that discussions of religion and faith is just not done in polite society. However, it is not a matter of poor etiquette to offer a solution and solace to those in pain or despair. Humanists should just as readily offer assistance to someone in despair or hurtful situations of life when the humanist holds the means of assistance and hope. Christians are not imposing their views on anyone but sharing the difference Jesus has made in their lives and care enough about others to want their lives to be similarly transformed.

2. How does the Christian respond to the humanist that chastises Christians for presuming the Christian faith is superior to other faiths when all faiths lead to the same God? (183-184)

The Christian must point out that all faiths are not the same and all faiths do not lead to God. One of the purposes of faith or religion is to answer the basic questions of life, and Christianity is the only worldview that leads to order in one's soul and society because it is based on eternal truths about God, the universe, and man's place therein. Humanists are disingenuous when they equate Christianity with all other faiths because humanists deny a Creator in the first place. Humanists use this tactic because they wish to destroy or at least drive Christianity from the public square by attempting to erase all distinctions between Christianity and other religions in their demand for a simplistic, non-demanding religion in which all religions lead to the same God. Humanists then indict Christianity for the failures of other religions with false worldviews in bringing answers to life's basic questions.

3. How and why do humanists promote the dualism of faith and society? (184)

Humanists promote the concept of dualism (separation) of faith and the public square. Private faith is tolerated as long as it receives no illumination in the public square. For the humanist it is a means whereby faith will be allowed to die a natural death having been successfully driven from the public square and limited in its exposure to following generations. The dualism of a private faith separated from the public square should not be seen as a humanist endorsement of faith but merely as a tactic of suppression.

4. Under what banner do Humanists promote the dualism of faith and society? (184-185)

For the secular humanist, pluralism demands all religion be removed from the public square, but this is a different interpretation of pluralism than held by Americans of the Revolutionary era. The correct definition of a pluralistic society is one "…in which members of diverse ethnic, racial, religious, or social groups maintain an autonomous participation in and development of their traditional culture or special interest *within the confines of a common civilization.*" Although it exhibited a form of pluralism that denied government interference with their beliefs, America's *common civilization* during the Revolutionary era also exhibited an exceptionally strong religious sanction which was the "…power of Christian teaching over private conscience [that] made possible the American democratic society."

5. When Tocqueville arrived in the United States in 1830, he was struck by the religious atmosphere which he attributed to the separation of church and state. How was that separation of church and state different from the humanists' "wall of separation" used to drive Christianity from the public square? (185)

He found the spirit of religion and the spirit of freedom "…intimately linked together in *joint reign* over the same land." When the Founders wrote the Constitution, they weren't "fixing" and "insuring" religious freedom but preserving it. They were *not* building a wall to restrain religion and its influence in the public square. To the former colonists, religion in America was separate in that it was the overarching cover, the center to which one looked in the times of political turmoil, the anchor to which citizens held in times of national peril. Christianity reigns without obstacles by universal consent…the result is that in the world of morality everything is definite and settled, although the world of politics is given over to debate and human experiment."

6. How do we reconcile Tocqueville's "separation of church and state" with his "reign of the spirit of religion over the land"? (186-187)

Tocqueville succinctly articulated the feelings of the Founding Americans (the majority of Americans of the era, not just the Founding fathers) when he wrote, "Religion, which never interferes directly in the government of Americans, should therefore be regarded as the first of their political institutions, for, if it does not give them the taste for liberty, it enables them to take unusual advantage of it." Therefore, on the one hand we have a separation of church and state while on the other hand we have the moral force of Christianity and Christian teaching that operates on private conscience. This joint reign made possible American democratic society.

7. Given that America is a nation of immigrants, compare and contrast the moral suasion of the Christian faith with the leveling practices of the humanistic philosophy in bringing unity and cohesion to the nation. (188)

The moral suasion of the Christian faith worked through the individual and family to bring stability and unity to the nation as opposed to enforcement by the state. Yet, the modern secular humanist looks to the hammer of the state to preserve and stabilize America through a myriad of divisive policies, edicts, and laws designed to level society in accordance with humanist theory and practice. The cost of such leveling is a loss of unity, purpose, and vision. There is no center to which the nation may look to gain its bearings or anchor to restrain the ship of state as it is beset by the storm of political and human avarice in the conduct of the nation's affairs.

8. What is the premise behind the humanists' leveling practice of multiculturalism? (189)

The multicultural movement in schools is premised on the belief that America is too immersed in Western "Eurocentric" teachings to the detriment of other cultures. Thus, the education curriculum must be redirected to various counterculture teachings (such as Afrocentrism, humanistically defined feminism, homosexual teachings, and radical doctrines such as neoMarxism) that challenge the "white, male-dominated European studies." The attack on Western civilization comes through a dismissal of American religious values as they intersected with and made possible the rise of the American political system. Alternatively, multiculturalists promote humanistic philosophers and their adherents such as Rousseau, Hobbes, Locke, Nietzsche, Freud, Marx, and Dewey, most of whom had little to nothing to do with American liberty.

9. What is the essence of multiculturalism? (190)

The essence of multiculturalism has its roots in the denial of absolutes, one of the cardinal doctrines of humanism, which translates into a moral relativism. Such a values free approach, according to the humanists, makes it impossible to judge one period or era in relation to another or to say that one culture's ethic is superior or inferior to another. Therefore, we must agree that all belief systems are "…coexisting and equally valid." Thus, multiculturalism is merely a subset of the larger humanistic doctrine of cultural relativism and its corollary, tolerance. In the humanistic worldview, cultural relativism requires a suspension of judgment since all belief systems contain some truth within while no one belief system has all the truth.

10. Why has the growth of the Christianity been so successful around the world given that it is supposedly forcing various groups into a cultural straitjacket? (191)

The short answer is that Christianity is the truth and therefore provides the answers to life's basic questions and is a worldview that gives order

53

to one's soul. Christians understand that God created all peoples, but those people have developed different cultures and worldviews. But long before the proffering of theories by humanistic philosophers as to man's origin, the Judeo-Christian ethic recognized the common origin of man as described in Genesis of the Old Testament and in the New Testament when Paul spoke to the assembled Athenians of the God of the Hebrews that "…made of one blood all nations of men for to dwell on the face of the earth…"

11. Summarize what Richard Weaver believed regarding how culture develops, how it operates, and what must it do to survive. (192-193)

How culture develops – Culture is a product of the collective consciousness of a group seeing certain felt needs, "…a complex of values polarized by an image or idea." The group's dissatisfactions with the way things are results in an ordering process, a way of looking at the world as it should be. The very foundation of the cultural concept is unity that presupposes a general commonality of thought and action.

How culture operates – As a culture is formed and begins ordering its world to bring the satisfactions for which it was created, directions must be imposed on its members. These directions, limits, and required behaviors radiate through a center of authority with a subtle and pervasive pressure to conform. This pressure may range from cultural peer pressure to moral and legal restraints. Those that do not conform are repelled of necessity. Thus, in any culture there are patterns of inclusion and exclusion. Without such patterns, the culture is unprotected and disintegrates over time. The intrinsic nature of culture compels that it be exclusive rather than all inclusive, a concept of almost heretical proportions for the secular humanist.

How cultures fail – Cultures fail and disintegrate without the power to reject that which does not adhere to its central force. Cultures also fail over time if they adopt worldviews that are inadequate to answer life's basic questions.

12. How does one reconcile tolerance in society and a culture's need for exclusivity? (193)

Tolerance suggests acceptance and inclusiveness while exclusivity implies segregation and denial. By segregation is not meant segregation *within* a culture but *between* cultures. It is in the humanistic definition of pluralism that cultures are prone to failure. By its very essence, culture must discriminate against those outside its boundaries that do not share its central vision. A culture must believe in its uniqueness, worth, and the superiority of its worldview. To attempt to meld together or comingle multiple cultures into one culture with multiple centers of vision is to create a powerless culture with little influence and place it on the road to disintegration. By definition, culture must be an inward-looking vision and resist the alien. Without such is a loss of wholeness, and culture's cohesiveness dissolves into chaos as its various parts drift into orbits of parochial interests and egocentrism.

13. At what point must a pluralistic society suspend tolerance and act in opposition to a rival culture? (194)

That point is reached and pluralism defended when a rival culture attributes immanence to its forms, i.e., attempts to replace the pre-existing pluralistic society's central vision.

14. Compare and contrast the Christian and humanist basis for morality. (195-196)

The proponent of the Judeo-Christian ethic claims that the moral basis for its worldview rests on a host of intelligible sources such as the permanent things, the universal truths perceived by mankind, the revelation of God to the Hebrews and the world, and the impact of Christ and the apostles—the sum total of man's experiences, both negative and positive, passed down from generation to generation since time immemorial.

Humanists believe that because we are social animals morality results from our innate altruism, a moral instinct of selflessness although not equally developed in all humans. The origin of man's morality evolved from his ability to connect value or benefit with behaving well toward others. Human need resulted in a moral code, and "…codes of behavior in society come from our social agreements, our social construct of morals that benefit us all."

Chapter 14 – Government – "…America is not a Christian nation"

1. If President Obama does not consider America a Christian nation, Jewish nation, or a Muslim nation, what values does he see as guiding the nation? (200)

Secular values that are respectful of religious freedom, respectful of the rule of law, respectful of freedom.

2. How does the author counter President Obama's assertion that we are guided by secular values? (200)

The United States is a nation founded upon Judeo-Christian beliefs. We are a nation whose majority professes Christianity and believes America is a Christian nation.

3. In his 2006 speech regarding his vision for America, what does President Obama believe that democracy demands of the religiously motivated and what is his justification for his belief? (201)

"Democracy demands that the religiously motivated translate their concerns into universal, rather than religion-specific, values… I cannot simply point to the teachings of my church or evoke God's will. I have to explain why abortion violates some principle that is accessible to people of all faiths, including those with no faith at all…Politics depends on our ability to persuade each other of common aims based on a common reality. It involves the compromise. At some fundamental level, religion does not allow for compromise…To base one's life on such uncompromising commitments may be sublime, but to base our policy making on such religious commitments would be a dangerous thing…"

4. How do secular humanists use Thomas Jefferson's "wall of separation between church and state" to drive Christianity from the institutions of American life? (202-204)

Jefferson's phrase has been lifted out of context and incorrectly applied it to the establishment clause of the First Amendment in their efforts to ban all religion and religious expression from the public arena. Some now erroneously call the establishment clause the "separation clause."

5. What is the correct interpretation of the establishment clause and Jefferson's "wall of separation"? (202-203, 202n-203n)

The First Amendment prohibition dealt with the establishment of a *preferred* religion, i.e., a state sponsored religion. It also prohibited the meddling of the federal government into the free exercise of religion. The purpose of Jefferson's remarks was to address the concerns of the Danbury Baptist Association with regard to a rumor that one denomination would become the official national church *as opposed* to the secularists' ideal of a total separation of church from state. His response was to assure the Baptist group that the government would not establish any one denomination as the national denomination. Jefferson's wall was to be one way and meant to protect the Church from the government and not the government from the Church.

6. What is the evidence that supports the fact that the United States was founded upon Christian principles? (206)

The principles of the Hebraic-Christian tradition are woven throughout the Constitution, the Bill of Rights, first laws, and other founding documents that govern the land and demonstrate that the Founders were heavily reliant on biblical principles. However, one must look not only at the founding documents but also at the complete history of the lives of the Founders, and their actions, words, and deeds as well as the history of the colonies since Jamestown was established in 1607. It is by a distillation of the history of the entire colonial period and founding era that one can discern the Christian principles over-arching the newly formed United States.

7. In the Supreme Court case, *Holy Trinity v. United States, 1892*, what was the court's conclusion with regard to the obligation to govern by Christian principles and to oppose enactment and enforcement of laws contrary to those principles? (208)

Following numerous examples from Columbus down to the Declaration of Independence which included portions forty-four state constitutions that affirm the religious nature and Christian character of the American people, the court said,

> There is no dissonance in these declarations. There is a universal language pervading them all, having one meaning; they affirm and reaffirm that this is a religious nation. These are not individual sayings, declarations of private persons: they are organic utterances; they speak the voice of the entire people... 'Christianity, general Christianity, is and always has been a part of the common law...not Christianity with an established church...but Christianity with liberty of conscience to all men.'... 'The people of this State, in common with the people of this country, profess the general doctrines of Christianity, as the rule of their faith and practice... we are a Christian people, and the morality of the country is deeply engrafted upon Christianity, and not upon the doctrines or worship of those impostors [other religions].

8. What is the Christian's answer to the secularist who says that the principles upon which the nation is governed should be religion neutral as only a secular worldview can provide, i.e., a safe, religion free alternative? (209-210)

Secularism in itself is another worldview that deserves no special place or role in governance. Secularism is its own faith—a faith that denies God or at the least banishes God to remain behind the closed doors of a silent church or in the muzzled confines of one's heart. More importantly, the secular society will ultimately become highly disordered and miserable in its existence. It is a breeding ground for divisiveness and tribalism. No overtly secular society in history has been successful in maintaining religious freedom over the long term.

9. What did William Blackstone believe with regard to the laws of society? (211)

All of a society's laws must be subject to the authority of a higher law dictated by God Himself. The law of nature is binding in all the earth, in all countries, and at all times. No human laws are of any validity, if contrary to the higher law; and such of human laws as are valid derive all their force and all their authority from the higher law.

Chapter 15 – Government – Liberalism and Progressivism in America

1. What was the political legacy of the Enlightenment and how does it differ from the Christian worldview? (213)

To understand the pervasive humanism and secularism in America, one must understand liberalism. Liberalism was the political legacy of the Enlightenment. The difference between liberalism and the Judeo-Christian ethic revolves around a disagreement on the end purpose of man. For the humanist, the focus of life is on self and the happiness of man. In the Christian worldview, the focus is relationship with God on this planet and for eternity.

2. Describe the skeptical revolutionary cultural tradition that emanated from the age of Enlightenment? (213)

The Enlightenment "...promoted the belief that critical and autonomous human reason held the power to discover the truth about life and the world, and to progressively liberate humanity from the ignorance and injustices of the past."

3. As the secularization of American society occurred between 1870 and 1930, how did evangelical Protestant Christianity respond? (214)

A tenuous compromise developed between evangelical Protestant Christianity and Enlightenment liberalism. Amid the rising skepticism, positivism, and Darwinism emanating from Enlightenment liberalism, the new liberal and modernists Protestant leaders chose survival through accommodation with the adversary and their doctrines of Science, Progress, Reason, and Liberation. But this compromise would only forestall the approaching "...final dominance of Enlightenment moral order in the public square and the relegation of Christian and other religious concerns to private life" that has gained increasing momentum since the 1930s.

4. What is the difference between the liberalism at the founding of the United States and the creation of its Constitution and that of contemporary liberalism? (214)

Liberalism at the founding was based on beliefs in "…religious freedom, political equality, constitutional democracy, the rule of law, limited government, private property, the market economy, and human rights." However, contemporary liberals champion vast government-run programs involving health, education, and welfare; affirmative action programs for minorities and women; prohibition of discrimination based on sexual orientation; legalization of same-sex marriages; legalized abortion and government funding of abortion for women with inadequate financial means; and opposition to the death penalty.

5. What are the two supports upon which the contemporary liberal rests? (24-215)

The first support is an activist government that proactively identifies real or perceived economic or social injustice and designs and implements programs to attack the various forms of injustice. The second support of contemporary liberalism is the advancement of a "personal liberationist's" agenda that rejects traditional norms of morality (generally dealing with sexuality, life, and death) and laws that enforce or promote those traditional norms.

6. Why does liberalism's concern for the individual (dignity of the individual, freedom of speech, and equal rights before the law) divorced from the Judeo-Christian ethic rest on a fallacy? (215)

Liberalism's concern for the individual is divorced from tradition and religion and consequently is shackled by the power of the state and therefore results in the devaluation of the individual.

7. According to Russell Kirk, liberalism contains four universal articles of faith. Summarize each of these. (214-215)

Affectation of change – The liberal's chant for change is a matter of principle and reflects a doctrinaire hatred for permanence.

Exaltation of the individual – Results in self-centeredness; hence, selfishness becomes virtue. For the liberal, community is secondary to a pervasive individualism where individual, personal rights are supreme. Duty and obligation to clan and community are consigned to the dustbin of a foolish and irrelevant past.

Discard tradition and its foundations – Liberals envision themselves with a mandate to remake the world by discarding tradition and destroying the foundations upon which such traditions rest. Such a remaking of the world must dispense with constraints of justice and order.

Progress – Liberals advance the idea of progress in which mankind, with no aid from a supernatural God, is getting better and better. Through enlightened self-interest and private judgment the present is presumed to be far superior to the past, and the future will be better still.

8. How is conservatism both different from and not the opposite of liberalism? (216)

Unlike liberalism, conservatism is not an ideology encompassing a sociopolitical program of continuously changing assertions, theories, and aims—a thing invented by the mind of man. Rather, conservatism: avows that there exists a transcendent moral order in which man and his society ought to conform; upholds social continuity which has produced order, justice, and freedom over many centuries; relies on the principle of prescription—adherence to things established by immemorial usage including rights and morals; and recognizes the imperfectability of man and therefore the impossibility of creating a perfect social order.

9. What is the foundational concept underpinning liberalism and ultimately humanism? (217)

Progressivism is the concept of human perfectibility and is to be achieved through growth of scientific knowledge and growth of industry which are unaffected by human endeavor as progress is inevitable.

10. Contrast a liberal's progressivism and a conservative's prescription for order in society? (218-219)

For the liberal, progress is a top-down affair—society to individual man. Social engineers and planners adjust and tweak society so that man might improve. Progressivism is a child of humanism and places its faith in mankind's ability to solve his own problems. Those solutions will be achieved through far reaching social programs resting upon a complete social implementation of reason and scientific method. By contrast, the conservative understands that man must achieve order of the soul before society can achieve order. Individual man must return to a right relationship with God, a state of being rather than becoming, and this right relationship brings order to the soul. As man orders his soul, so too will society achieve order.

11. How does the humanists' exaltation of the dignity and preciousness of the individual (5th principle of Humanist Manifesto II) conflict with the humanist commitment to some form of the greatest-happiness-for-the-greatest-number principle which they consider the highest moral obligation to humanity as a whole? (220-221)

The humanist proposes that the individual's dignity and preciousness is found in an individual's freedom. Yet, there appears a fundamental conflict in the statements of humanists with regard to the individual and the larger society. Under the humanist philosophy it is evident that the individual must be subordinate to the good of all humanity, and it is the leaders of the state that determine the definition of what is good. All reflect a top-down form of viewing and organizing society with the individual being the down portion of the equation. Therefore, with the individual's loss of freedom in a humanistic society, so comes the loss of dignity and preciousness of the individual.

12. How do those holding the Judeo-Christian ethic view the individual? (222)

It was the Judeo-Christian ethic that reduced the power of the state and simultaneously raised the individual. For man is God's creation, but man's specialness lies in his inherent individual worth because he was created in God's image, possesses an immortal soul, and journeys on the path of redemption that will lead to an eternal relationship with his creator. Thus, man's allegiance is to God and transcends the bonds of earth and time. We speak no more of mass man but of the human person who God loves. Biblical individualism presented a new limit to earthly powers.

13. According to Richard Weaver, what are the three ways humanists attempt to devalue or demote man? (223)

Insignificance of man – Humanists point to man's insignificant in relation to the vastness of the universe, and therefore man is presumed to be insignificant and unimportant to the supposed Creator. In other words, importance is based on size or location. In the biblical view, value is imputed by the creator, not his creation, and the value of man to the Creator is enormous when one considers the cost of man's redemption.

Diminished worth of man – Darwin's theory of evolution diminishes the worth of man. No longer the center of creation, man was robbed of his special origins, the divine spark snuffed out, and was now counted among the animal kingdom and therefore shares a common ancestry with other creatures that struggled out of the primeval ooze.

Loss of free will – Man was robbed of his free will, and his actions are now explained by material causality. He is now brute beast, a slave to animal passions, and those actions can be predicted and explained by materialistic determinism. Man only reacts to material, physical stimuli the same as might a laboratory rat or Pavlov's dog. Therefore, mechanistic man has no spirit, but this denial of a free will runs contrary to the intuitive consensus of all mankind.

14. What has been the definition of freedom through the ages and why does man choose to place some limits on that freedom? (223-224)

Freedom has always meant an absence of restraint or domination of the individual. Freedom operates where the individual is free to act or choose and not be subject to force or threat. However, freedom is akin to fire in the sense that unbridled freedom or licentiousness allows irresponsibility and destroys. In other words, one's personal liberty must not become oppression or harm to another. However, man desires order and organizes himself in society to achieve a measure of freedom. To achieve order and therefore make possible a measure of freedom, he must surrender some of his freedom and this surrender involves controlling his appetites and passions.

15. Compare and contrast the biblical and humanist views of freedom. (224-225)

Humanistic concepts vest the primacy of freedom with the group, not the individual. The importance of the group as opposed to the individual is confirmed by reading excerpts from *Humanist Manifesto I* and *II*. In the humanist philosophy, freedom is not a state of being but rather something that is created and fastened to the so-called *greater good of all humanity* and thus has become adulterated. Under humanists' assault, freedom has lost its meaning and becomes a tool for the conditioners to mold society by group coercion as opposed to individual choice.

The moral suasion of Christianity operates at the individual level. It influences or persuades but does not command as does humanism. Christ instructs his followers to share the good news through evangelism, but a close reading of the New Testament yields an incontrovertible picture of Christianity as a non-coercive presentation of the gospel of Jesus Christ. Secular humanists wrongly perceive the sharing of the good news of Jesus Christ as being coercive, but such perceived coercion is contrary to the theme of the entire Bible and contrary to the Judeo-Christian doctrine of free will.

16. Define democracy—what it is and what it is not. (226-227)

Democracy is not an end but a means and can be fallible and uncertain. Democracy is not a synonym for freedom but a device to safeguard internal peace and individual freedom. Democracy must not be the source of power. Rather, it must be guided by fixed rules such as a constitution or it becomes arbitrary.

17. How have humanists redefined democracy to further their humanistic goals for society? (227)

Humanists have endowed democracy with intrinsic moral principles, something of value in and of itself. These moral principles are defined in such a way to support the humanist worldview of democracy: humanist definitions of liberty and equality, concern for the worth and dignity of the individual, recognition of an individual's right to do what he wishes and limits undue interference with his individual choice and action, provision of opportunity for growth and personal realization, tolerance of diversity, and enlargement of our discovery and insight. Therefore, if one opposes the humanists' moral principles that define democracy, then one opposes democracy in that it is undue interference with individual choice and action (e.g., abortion or euthanasia). Consequently, if one believes the Bible is the source of unchanging and God-given truth, then one opposes democracy for the humanist definition of democracy states that no individual or group may possess all the truth.

18. What is the difference between equality and fraternity as it relates to a culture? (229)

Fraternity is critical to a culture's survival. A viable culture must have a network of sentiment that looks toward a central vision. The network of sentiment implies feelings toward that central vision resulting in an adherence to the common body of beliefs of the group. Therefore, culture must reside on the foundation of fraternity which is other-directed and implies common purpose. Fraternity goes immeasurably deeper in history and long antedates equality. Equality is self-directed whereas fraternity is unifying and smoothes the way in preservation of culture. Unsentimental equality is fragmentary and divisive in its futile attempts at a mechanistic leveling of the elements of culture and leads to disintegration.

19. Why will the humanist's ideal of equality never achieve social harmony? (229-230)

The pursuit of equality has resulted in the identification of an ever expanding array of social problems demanding governmental attention and a resulting creation of "illusory rights" supposedly on par with the original Bill of Rights. In the quest for equality, these new rights must be addressed by a redistribution of social, political, and economic power that not only raises some but pushes others down. Two problems occur. First, Government cannot fix everything due to limited resources. Second, Americans see preferential treatment of certain groups as unfairly impinging on other individuals, something they find disquieting and somehow contrary to tenets upon which the nation was founded. Ultimately, social harmony unravels as government disappoints those seeking new levels of equality because it cannot fulfill the multiplying demands while at the same time government alienates the remainder of society that perceives it as acting unfairly in awarding preferential treatment.

20. What was the fallacy of the eighteenth century philosophers' democratic ideas of human equality? (230-231)

The idea of human equality flowed from the false humanistic assumption of the perfectibility of man. For what men are comes from experience. Therefore, men are equal at birth, and differences and inequalities arise due to environment. The solution is education that will result in an ideal democratic society. These ideas of human goodness were advanced by the philosophies of the rationalistic Enlightenment. The French revolutionaries adopted the optimistic but false doctrine of human goodness as opposed to the American Founders' reliance on a biblical view of man.

21. What was the equality proposed by John Adams and the other founders? (231-232)

All men are born to equal rights (moral and political equality—equality before God and the law) but *not* to equal powers, facilities, influence in society, and equal property and advantages. Adams said to teach otherwise is a "gross fraud."

22. Having failed to provide equality of income through political equality, what were the new demands of humanists and what were the tactics used to achieve their goals? (232-233)

Humanist levelers of society demanded economic democracy which meant a move from equality of opportunity to equality of outcome. Demands for economic democracy resulted in the creation of synthetic rights in which the government was supposed to respond to the newly defined inequalities. As the legislative, executive and judicial branches of government enacted remedies for the newly defined inequalities, the synthetic rights gained permanency and became legal rights.

23. Describe the concept of justice and its connection to order and freedom. (233-235)

Justice is a universal truth, a thing of permanence that transcends the whole of man's time on this planet and pertains to all cultures. Justice refers to the ideals of fairness, impartiality, and right action. Justice is one of the three fundamental virtues that forms the bond that unites American society, the other two being order and freedom. Order is the first need of a society. As a society recognizes certain principles of a tolerable civil order, justice is possible and enforceable. Justice becomes the critical link between indispensable order and the elixir of freedom. A just society requires a standard of judgment by which fairness, impartiality, and right action is measured, and this standard of judgment must be above the temper of the moment. This standard of judgment is the law which follows established principles and is no respecter of rank or station. For America those established principles flowed from the English common law that arose over centuries of judicial decisions and was derived from the experience of people living in community and settling their differences by legal means over a very long period of time. Much of common law flowed from natural law, a set of norms that derive from an authority above the state.

24. How have humanists redefined justice to fit their worldview? (234)

Justice for the humanist derives *not* from the long centuries of human interaction that created standards of fairness, impartiality, and right action. For the humanist, man is an economic being. "All social values –liberty and opportunity, income and wealth, and the bases of self-respect– are to be distributed equally unless an unequal distribution of any, or all of these values is to everyone's advantage…The legitimacy for such a society is not a god, or the rule of a king, or even the rule of a powerful clique. It is as if *we construct* society according to an imaginary contract that all rational citizens could have made. Justice means that there is a fair measure of economic distribution."

Chapter 16 – Government – Humanism and the Rise of Socialism

1. How are the humanist philosophy and socialism linked? (237-238)

The political framework for the imposition of the humanistic concepts of order, justice, freedom, and equality is socialism. The critical importance of a socialistically organized society to the imposition of tenets of humanism are reflected by excerpts from Humanist Manifestoes I and II: A *socialized and cooperative economic order must be established* to the end that the equitable distribution of the means of life be possible. The world community must engage in *cooperative planning* concerning the use of rapidly depleting resources. We need to democratize the economy and judge it by its responsiveness to human needs, testing results in terms of the common good.

2. Socialism as a foundation for modern collectivist governments originated when and where, and what was the underlying fallacy upon which it was based? (238-239)

Socialism as a basis for modern collectivist governments arose from the philosophy of Rousseau in France during the eighteenth century. Under his Social Contract, all men must consent and be bound to the will of the majority. The basic fallacy of Rousseau's Social Contract theory rests upon his belief in the goodness of man as opposed to his fallen nature. Lacking safeguards for the man's intrinsically corrupt nature, the freedom of individuals and minorities are trounced by the despotic majority. Rousseau and other French philosophers and revolutionaries began with an invented virtue for man who was endowed with and aware of his abstract rights which society owed him. He was also clear about duties that welded him to society—liberty, equality, and fraternity. Edmund Burke accused the French of failing to consider history and traditions of the past as well as the corrupt nature of man.

3. What was the essence of the Communist Manifesto written by Marx and Engels in 1848? (241)

The essence of the Manifesto appears in Section II and calls for the abolition of private property, the family, and ultimately countries and nationalities. The proletarians, wage laborers who have no means of production of their own, would rule. Once in power, the national differences and antagonisms between people would vanish through united action leaving only good government or administration.

4. What does the author suggest is the true end result of the socialist's lofty and altruistic goals of justice, equality, and security? (242)

The altruistic and lofty goals of socialism become somewhat tarnished when one examines a society under the growing influence of socialism: freedom becomes slavery, prosperity erodes to poverty, equality descends to mediocrity, and security dissolves into boredom.

5. According to Hayek, how do the levelers sell socialism when it implicitly requires a limit on the strongest political motive— the urge for freedom? (242)

The levelers promise a *new* freedom in place of the old. Throughout history freedom always meant freedom from coercion, freedom from the arbitrary power of other men, and release from the ties which left the individual no choice but obedience to the orders of a superior to whom he was attached. However, the *new* freedom promised by the levelers of society was to be a freedom from necessity, a release from the compulsion of the circumstances which inevitably limit the range of choice of all of us, that is, the "despotism of physical want" had to be broken and the "restraints of the economic system relaxed."

6. In practical terms, what is the end result of the imposition on society of this new freedom? (243)

The new freedom is merely another name for leveling society through an equal distribution of wealth. Rather than expanding the range of choice, leveling results in a greater limitation on choice. In practical terms, the new freedom is socialism which "means the elimination of private enterprise, of private ownership of the means of production, and the creation of a system of 'planned economy' in which the entrepreneur working for profit is replaced by a central planning body."

7. Describe the beginnings of the social gospel movement in the United States and the end result thereof. (243-244)

The reform movement in the United States began during the last two decades of the 1800s. The leadership of the movement consisted of men and women of wealth and influence and included many from the mainstream Christian denominations with secular leanings who saw man as inherently perfectible but held back from that perfect state by his environment. The efforts of these men and women to fix man's environment became the social gospel movement which had strong ties to humanism and socialism. The social gospeler successfully appropriated the role filled by the Christian church for centuries and then quickly marginalized if not entirely eliminated its core beliefs and teachings as the process became secularized. The social gospel movement, headed primarily by mainstream Protestant ministers, switched the emphasis from perfecting the inner man to social justice.

8. How does Richard Weaver describe the humanists' view of property and what is his response thereto? (248)

Weaver writes that, "Almost every trend of the day points to an identification of right with the purpose of the state and that, in turn, with the utilitarian greatest material happiness for the greatest number." Weaver argues that private property is the last metaphysical right remaining because it does not depend on some measure of social usefulness that can be bent to the greatest good for the greatest number. State control of the material elements of a society positions it to allow the denial of freedom, but private property and personal income stands as a bulwark and provides a "…sanctuary against pagan statism." The biblical worldview through its imposition of boundaries on the power of the state consequentially supports and encourages economic freedom and subsequently free-market economies because the power of government to dictate or interfere with private transactions is limited.

9. How did the Supreme Court's liberal interpretation in 1936 of the "general welfare" clause of the Constitution encroach on fundamental property rights? (249)

This liberal interpretation significantly expanded what the legislature could do with regard to providing for the "general welfare" of the citizens of the United States and became an unprecedented assault on right of private property through imminent domain laws, a diminution of the right of contract and obligations there under, an oppressive income tax system, and the onerous limitations on the possession and use of private property through regulation.

10. How does Charles Murray describe transformation of a free society into a socialistic society with massive government intrusion into almost every aspect of an individual's life and the end result thereof? (257-258)

Murray states that the totality of life, the "stuff of life" as he calls it, revolves around four institutions: family, community, vocation, and faith. As America encouraged personal success in each of these areas, the nation thrived. The past American *encouragement* of success in each of these institutions was contrasted with the European *support* that each of these same institutions received over many years through advanced socialism. The support given by European socialism has undermined those institutions and usurped the responsibilities formerly in the province of the individual and consequently "…sapped much of the energy, drive, and satisfaction from living."

Chapter 17 – Science – Naturalistic Evolution

1. What is naturalism? (259)

Humanism's gospel is naturalism, and its tenets of faith insist that human beings, the earth, and the unending universe of space and time are all parts of one great Nature. Existence and Nature are one and the same, and apart from Nature nothing exists. An explanation of everything that exists can be obtained through observation of the forces of nature. In the naturalistic explanation, the universe was an endless and unbroken series of causes and effects through time.

2. Describe Charles Darwin's theory of evolution and the impact thereof. (260-261)

Darwin's theory of evolution rests on three concepts. The first deals with descent with modification. Darwin proposed that the species were not immutable. Rather, species were capable of or susceptible to change over time, and new species have appeared by the process of descent with modification over long periods during the earth's history. The second proposition states that all life descended from one or just a few common ancestors. The third proposition states that the diversity of life flowing from the common ancestors was not haphazard or erratic but guided by a force called natural selection, more popularly known as "survival of the fittest." Naturalism and Darwinian evolution was a symbiotic relationship for the naturalistic worldview in explaining creation and was of critical importance for Darwinism. In Darwin's theory of evolution, humanists had found a weapon to not only sever the natural from the supernatural but to destroy the supernatural altogether.

3. How do evolutionists dismiss the extreme improbabilities of life beginning through *undirected* natural causes and why is their explanation unacceptable? (261-262)

For the evolutionist, the only alternative for life to exist is undirected and natural. Thus, for life to exist, it must have occurred that way regardless of the improbabilities. The evolutionists' answer is self-proving and therefore not acceptable.

4. Describe the theory of theistic evolution in which evolution is supposed to be God-governed but attempts to remain compatible with Darwinian evolution on scientific matters. What is the fallacy thereof? (262)

C. S. Lewis described those that believe "...the small variations by which life on this planet 'evolved' from the lowest forms to Man were not due to chance but to the 'striving' or 'purposiveness' of a Life-Force." Lewis equates Life-Force as something that must be with or without a mind. Either is fatal to theistic evolution. On the one hand, if the force is without a mind, it is cannot strive or have purpose. If it has a mind by which that life arose and moves to perfection, then the mind is really a God which is at odds with the Darwinian view.

5. What is the difference between macroevolution and microevolution? (263)

Microevolution occurs when small-scale variations occur within a kind. These small-scale changes arise from adaptability and natural selection, but such changes occur within a kind and do not create something new. Macroevolution supposedly occurs as small microevolutionary changes accumulate and result in a new species. However, macroevolutionists fail to provide scientific proof—the proverbial missing links.

6. How does the fossil record fail to support Darwin's theory of evolution?

Under Darwin's theory the great diversity of life present on the earth evolved from one or at most a few ancestors. As one species evolved to another, there would be transitional forms, e.g., half ape and half man. These transitional forms would provide a measure of proof for the Darwinian evolutionary process. The source of that proof is found only in the fossil record. However, the transitional types Darwin describes are not only missing from the present world but also missing from the fossil record. (264)

7. How do defenders of Darwin's theory use punctuated equilibrium to explain the lack of a fossil record? (265-266)

Darwin's gradualism is replaced by an evolutionary process (punctuated equilibrium) that happened in a short period of time, was caused by sudden changes in the environment, and was too quick to be reflected in the fossil record. These spurts of evolution would be followed by relatively long periods of stability. Neo-Darwinists generally reject punctuated equilibrium and attribute sudden appearance of species to various gap theories (mosaic evolution and stabilizing selection) in the fossil records. However, these theories are just as weak and inconsistent as Darwin's explanations and arguments in support of naturalistic evolution.

8. What is neo-Darwinism? (267)

During the first half of the twentieth century, Darwin's supporters in various fields of science (e.g., comparative anatomy, genetics, and embryology) began developing their respective definitions of what evolution was. Through a series of interdisciplinary meetings as mid-century approached, the leaders of the various fields attempted to develop a coherent theory of Darwinian evolution based on Darwin's principles. This "evolutionary synthesis" became the basis of modern evolutionary thought and was called neo-Darwinism. Neo-Darwinism was essentially non-molecular and did not account for modern biochemistry whose beginnings came after the neo-Darwinist initiatives.

9. Do mutations in DNA's genetic code support Neo-Darwinists reliance on random mutation and natural selection as the primary mechanism for evolution? (268)

A mutation results from an error in the copying commands of DNA's genetic code. Generally, mutations are at the very least harmful and can be fatal. An accumulation of these mutations leads to degeneration or retrograde evolution. But neo-Darwinists require that many thousands of rare but helpful or beneficial mutations must occur in a single organism and result in a new organ or structure. Not only must thousands of rare but helpful mutations occur, Darwinists believe favorable mutations occur because their environments "demand" such and therefore mutations are "directed" to provide a fix. However, mutations are random and are not related to the usefulness of that mutation. Therefore mutations in DNA's genetic code do not support reliance on random mutation and natural selection as the primary mechanism for evolution.

10. What is the concept of "irreducible complexity" and how does it pose significant problems for evolutionary theory? (269-270)

The concept of irreducible complexity applies to "...a single system composed of several well-matched, interacting parts that contribute to basic function, wherein the removal of any one of the parts causes the system to effectively cease functioning." An irreducibly complex system cannot be produced directly (that is, by continuously improving the initial function, which continues to work by the same mechanism) by slight, successive modifications of a precursor system, because any precursor to an irreducibly complex system that is missing a part is by definition non-functional." Darwinian evolution must account for the addition of complex organs in their entirety, not piecemeal through a long series of gradations in complexity. The evolution of complex systems through countless gradations of change won't work.

11. Given the mounting difficulties in the defense of naturalistic evolution, why is there such a massive and fierce defense of naturalistic evolution as "accepted fact"? (273)

At some point there is an end to the "explanatory chain" where scientific explanations must "have certain starting assumptions built in." Ultimately, the deep questions of existence "...will always lie beyond the scope of empirical science..." Where the explanatory chain ends, faith begins, and the scientist must leave science and its experiments, analyses, and hypotheses behind. For the humanist that faith begins with naturalism, and naturalism preaches that apart from nature nothing exists including a supernatural creator. It is a given, an accepted fact, but not provable by science. Without faith in the accepted fact of naturalism, evolution would not have a foundation. Thus, evolution too must rest on the humanist faith in naturalism.

12. How does Darwin's accepted fact of evolution differ from the accepted fact of evolution by modern day evolutionists? (274)

According to Darwin, if one accepts his details as accepted fact, then his general theory must be believed. For modern-day evolutionists the theory of evolution is accepted fact, and it is the details (mechanism and the appearance of new data) that must be worked out. In other words, for Darwin truth was in the details that supported belief in the general theory. When those indisputable details proved fallible, latter-day evolutionists point to the accepted fact of evolution with the promise that supporting details will be discovered.

Chapter 18 – Human Sciences and the Secularization of America

1. In the study and understanding of human nature, why has there been so little progress in sociology and psychology? (278)

The histories of these disciplines have been marked by attempts to avoid philosophical and theological assumptions that recognize the person as "...a whole being, having inner qualities that precise scientific theories cannot explain." This is why the two disciplines tend to reflect such little progress. New theories are constantly proposed to replace out-of-fashion fads and discredited theories. The disciplines will continue to go in circles and cycles until the subjects of personhood, human behavior, and relationships are looked upon from a biblical perspective and are not based on the assumptions put forth by social Darwinism.

2. During the last three decades of the 1800s, what was the impact of social Darwinism's capture of academia and mainstream religion through the social gospel movement? (279)

The tenuous compatibility between the teachings and beliefs of Christianity and the ends of socialism enabled the ascending leadership of the liberal Protestant denominations to successfully promote the social gospel, but secularizing forces ultimately appropriated the role filled by the Christian church for centuries. The secularization process quickly marginalized if not entirely eliminated Christianity's core beliefs and teachings as the social gospel movement, headed primarily by mainstream Protestant ministers, switched the emphasis from perfecting the inner man to social justice.

3. How did the champions of human sciences (psychology and sociology) such as John Dewey view the physical and human sciences? (280)

For the social Darwinists, there were no differences in the physical and human sciences. Integration of the doctrines and philosophies of physical and human sciences is made and applied as a single empirical, naturalistic scientific approach in addressing the needs of individuals and society.

4. How did Keith Meador describe the result of mainline Protestantism's choice not to fight but to compromise, accommodate, and acquiesce to the secularizing aspects of social Darwinism? (281)

Meador stated that, "In the 1920s, mainline Protestant seminaries began teaching the concept of 'self-realization,' which conceived of the self as an entity whose fulfillment and full potentiation were paramount within the spiritual life. As a result, helping people 'adjust' and 'adapt' in service of the self became the goal of pastoral care and counseling."

5. Why have psychologists failed for over a hundred years to gain a clear understanding of human nature? (284)

Naturalistic and humanistic psychologists have attempted to squeeze psychology into the mold of natural science and have rejected religious explanations of human nature. But without God in the equation, secular psychologists distort a clear understanding of human nature because science explores only natural processes and ignores "human realities" and questions of "…human meaning, purpose, and spiritual conditions."

6. What is the naturalistic sociologist's understanding of human behavior and the patterns of relationships by which people are connected in society, social institutions, and social relationships? (285)

Under naturalistic sociology, the behavior of human beings is believed to be subject to certain laws similar to natural physical properties and interactions. The socially determined actions of persons occur in response to the demands and expectations of society. People are not passive objects of social force but have choice, and therefore investigating social problems is paramount as opposed to patterns of natural science. Humanistic sociologists generally follow the work of Karl Marx and believe that "…society is composed of interacting persons in a complex dynamic relationship."

7. Why do the views of naturalistic sociology and humanistic sociology fail to adequately describe human nature? (286)

Naturalistic assumptions are compatible with the concept of the fallen nature of man (original sin) but not with the doctrines of creation and free will. Humanistic assumptions are compatible with the view of creative humanity but not with the truth of fallen nature of man and the inability of humans to provide their own salvation.

8. What is scientism and its tenets of belief? (287)

Scientism is the rational application of scientific theories and methods of the natural sciences to society and politics. Scientism would allow mankind to sweep away the ills of society including ignorance, poverty, war, hatred, and crime. Scientism took its cue from evolutionary biology and viewed man as an animal that evolved over the ages. Man and society could be studied, understood, manipulated, and improved. Man would no longer be limited by imaginary concepts of right and wrong as he is merely a bundle of instincts and urges. Learned responses were responsible for flaws in human nature, not moral corruption. No longer would the barometer of conscience be allowed to guide and restrain. Without a conscience, there was no need for moral reasoning and moral responsibility. And of the soul, enlightened man has no need.

Chapter 19 – American Education

1. How does the author view education and instruction as being different? (289)

A body of knowledge may be known by simple instruction, that is, by the transmission of facts and principles. However, education encompasses a far broader mission. Education not only may contain instruction but is training for a way of life. Training for life must involve recognition of the central authority—the central vision—the collective consciousness in which the world is viewed. For a culture to survive, its adherents must see its implicit and unique worth.

2. What does the author believe to be the dominant conflict in American education for the last one hundred years? (289)

It is the conflict between the beliefs and values upon which the nation was founded and the ascendant progressive theory of education.

3. Summarize eight aims of progressive education that Richard Weaver identifies as fundamentally different and in conflict with the core teachings and traditions of Western civilization as defined by the Judeo-Christian heritage? (289-290)

Under progressive education's aims and core teachings,

- There is no permanency to a body of knowledge, no fixed truths or final knowledge.
- The focus of education is to teach students as opposed to teaching knowledge.
- Students' desires dictate what subjects to study and the aspects thereof as well as the amount of time spent and timing of that study.
- The teacher relinquishes his/her role as the authority and becomes a leader whose purpose is to "… synchronize and cooperate with the work of the group."
- Competition and grades are considered injurious and prejudicial because they promote feelings of superiority and inferiority which are "undemocratic."

- Democracy requires sensory or activist (hands on) learning and must be on a level with intellectual learning. Thus, things of the mind should never be exalted over the senses.
- Progressive education emphasizes the greater use of hands on, concrete objects as opposed to education through symbols such as language and mathematics.
- Students will adjust themselves to the existing society specifically and to a society conceived as social democracy generally.

4. How did higher education in North America move from an unequivocally Christian enterprise in the late nineteenth century to a monolithic secular progressive education establishment in the last half of the twentieth century? (291)

The progressive reform era that arose between the 1870s and about 1930 made possible the progressive's usurpation of moral authority from religion through the human sciences and the social gospel. By the 1870s, the stage was also set for reform of the ideology, organization, and practice of education. As the end of the nineteenth century approached, "…the breach separating the universities and the churches widened suddenly, and culminated in the extraordinarily rapid and dramatic 'disestablishment' of conservative Protestantism from North American academic life between roughly 1890 and 1930…Progressives were confident that they could use science to discover the kind of individual needed for the new industrial democracy, and then apply to schools scientifically proven tools for creating that individual." Over the course of the next half century progressive intellectuals seized the reigns of public education and effectively marginalized religious discourse and influence which ultimately resulted in "…a secularized educational ideology and bureaucratized public school system…" except for a smattering of local religious practices.

5. What is meant by the progressives' emphasis on child-centeredness in education? (293-294)

"In the enlightenment tradition, progressives saw human nature as essentially good or neutral, rejecting the view of original sin…The child, in this view, develops naturally through reason and experience.

Child-centeredness thus locates the source of authority in the self and human nature, rather than in God and the Supernatural. Because human nature is good and because the child is innately programmed to develop naturally, education must nurture the intrinsic development and expression of child nature rather than break it or submit it to authority. This conception lies at the basis of modern primary education." Under the child-centeredness approach, education is based on "child nature" and focuses on the interests, abilities, and needs of a child.

6. What are the two reasons given by Craig Gay for the rapid and comprehensive secularization of American education in the twentieth century? (294-295)

First, insurgent secular-humanist ideology displaced the reigning conservative Protestantism at colleges and universities in North America. In the growing secular culture, conservative Protestant educators feared appearing illiberal or sectarian to those political and industrial power bases whose support was necessary. Additionally, conservative Protestant educators allowed the progressives to frame the arguments and methodologies for establishing biblical truth. The rise of the modern research university is Gay's second cause of the rapid secularization of life at North American colleges and universities. Within the confines of such institutions arose a number of secularizing factors. Gay notes the modern intellectual practices of criticism, analysis, redefinition, and re-articulation, and even of simplification promotes agnostic tendencies and threaten belief in an eternal and unchanging truth.

7. What is the Uncurriculum that Rob Koons believes prevails at most colleges and universities? (300)

Such an approach to curriculum design usually exhibits a general lack of required courses, structure, and systematic order in meeting core course requirements for liberal arts studies. Rather, the Uncurriculum allows an accumulation of a group of unconnected courses that meet a 'distribution' standard. An unstructured, smorgasbord approach to curriculum offerings gives students the illusion of choice, but the choice is among courses the faculty wishes to teach (generally related to their specialties) as opposed to required core courses. Therefore, faculty members can concentrate on research and publication from whence flow promotions, salary increases, prestige, and tenure. Their self-interests are defended through a chant of post-modern and multicultural ideals.

8. Describe the structure of a liberal education that stands in opposition to the scatter-shot approach of the Uncurriculum. (300)

A liberal education encourages students to think through the great questions of life in a systematic manner, with the great minds of the Western tradition as their guides and interlocutors." A liberal education means "…an ordering and integrating of knowledge for the benefit of the free person—as contrasted with technical or professional schooling…" A liberal education "…is intended to free us from captivity to time and place: to enable us to take long views, to understand what it is to be fully human—and to be able to pass on to generations yet unborn our common patrimony of culture."

9. What are the consequences of abandoning a liberal education for the Uncurriculum? (301)

Acquisition of unrelated details becomes an end in itself and results in a form of fragmentation of worldview. Fragmentation causes man to descend from the glorious heights from which one can clearly see truth to a forest of facts and minutia that hide truth and ultimately destroys within men's minds the concept that truth exists. This is called relativism in which selected facts are arranged to fit the desired outcome. When the desired outcome fails to materialize or falls victim to another fad or fashion, old facts are discarded and new facts are marshaled to support the new desired outcome. In the fragmented worldview, facts become truth and particular facts are counted as wisdom.

Chapter 20 – American Family – Marriage and Family

1. How does the author describe the hierarchical nature of relationships in the Christian worldview? (305)

For Christians, the primary nature of relationships is hierarchical (vertical)—God's being is shown by the Father-Son relationship and the relationship of Christ with the Church of which he is the head and we are the body. Because man was created in God's image, the hierarchical pattern of relationships is evident in various entities throughout history— marriage, family, community, nations, and the Kingdom of God. Hierarchy implies authority, superior and subordinate, order, and rank.

2. What is meant by humanistic egalitarianism? (306)

Humanistic egalitarianism means a belief in human equality with special emphasis on "social, political, and economic rights and privileges" and a focus on the removal of any inequalities among humankind.

3. How does the author describe the equalitarian nature of relationships in the humanistic worldview? (306)

Under the humanistic worldview, equality has become a rapacious egalitarianism that imposes regimentation and leveling of circumstance which results in *unnatural* social groupings. One senses the relentless gravity of the humanistic worldview pulling society downward from hierarchy into a flat (horizontal) social plain and consequent mediocrity.

4. What are the consequences of modern society's loss of hierarchy? (305-306)

A loss of hierarchy in relationships occurs in modern society as it embraces the humanistic perversion "...that in a just society there are no distinctions." Loss of hierarchy leads to a loss of cultural center and ultimately society's disintegration. In reality, humanistic equalitarianism is a thief of status, property, patrimony, and ultimately freedom. And the most dangerous idea of modern society is an undefined equalitarianism which pretends to be the champion of justice but is the opposite. In such is not found justice.

5. Describe fraternity/brotherhood and its importance to society. (306-307)

"The ancient feeling of brotherhood carries obligations of which equality knows nothing. It calls for respect and protection, for brotherhood is *status* in family, and family is by nature hierarchical. It places people in a network of sentiment, not of rights." Cultures and societies must rest upon codes of behavior, and therefore they rely on fraternity and not equality. Fraternity resonates through history as it is the offspring of the seminal purposes of man— relationship with God and other men. The object of fraternity is other-directed and speaks of duty, congeniality, cooperation, and sense of belonging whereas equality focuses attention on self and results in egotism. Equality, rightly applied, is equality before God and the law.

6. Describe the family structure and its place in the world. (307-308)

The family structure is a societal institution established by the Creator. The family structure consisting of "…a father, mother and children living together in bonds of committed caring is not an arbitrary happenstance; nor is it mere convention that can be dismissed when it has outlived its usefulness." This ordered family structure is a part of the human constitution and is ingrained in man's nature in all of its facets—biological, emotional, social and moral. This structure allows for variety but sets definite boundaries, i.e., lines that cannot be crossed without being in opposition to the structured order of the family.

7. How does the author describe the highest form of the modern nuclear family? (309)

The highest form occurs when marriage is a freely chosen, exclusive, and permanent arrangement between a man and a woman that is a repository of sexual and emotional intimacy, affection, and friendship. Within this institution of monogamous marriage, children are conceived, born, loved, disciplined, nurtured, and raised. This is a reflection of the relationship God intended between Himself and humankind.

8. How has marriage remained a cultural universal while being changed and shaped over man's history? (310)

Marriage is a cultural universal because of man's very nature. Men and women are a "pair-bonding" species, and from such come reproduction and nurturance. Parents shape the moral understanding, behavior, feeling, and worldview of their children, and the family is where the generational transmission of moral and cultural values takes place. The home was the basic organizing unit of humankind—a father, mother, and children living together in bonds of committed caring. This was the basic structure. However, over man's history the molding and shaping of marriage and family progressed through human experience, economic considerations, accumulated wisdom, and moral enlightenment through revelation in the Old and New Testaments over the course of man's existence after the Fall. But these changes occurred without altering the cultural universal of the traditional nuclear family.

9. How do the cultural universals of marriage and family aid society? (310-311)

Society grew and stabilized through marriage and family and a network of extended family in which there are reciprocal expectations, obligations, and responsibilities. As two families celebrate the marriage and the consequent "entanglement" of the families, each family rises in status or affinity with the other as well as having reciprocal claims on each other. With status and affinity comes the motivator to right conduct by not bringing dishonor to the family. Another basic need of society is the establishment of rules for sexual conduct. The family supports monogamy between the husband and wife. To such is born children that have status as family. Without monogamy the family tends to dilution and disintegration through loss of legitimacy, social identity, legal recognition, cultural tradition, and an estate.

10. How did Christianity elevate the status of women in society? (311-312)

In Christianity, the marriage relationship was of such importance that it is described in terms of Christ's relationship with the church (his bride). With the new definition of marriage and family in the New Testament came a remarkable elevation in the status of women. Jesus' attitude and example during his earthly ministry became the definitive model for our understanding of male-female relationships, marriage, and family life. Both men and women were held accountable to the same standards of morality. The vows of marriage were meant to be permanent with divorce allowed under very limited circumstances.

11. Why has marriage between a man and woman been such a solemn and ritualistic occasion throughout history? (312)

The solemnity of the occasion arises from the enormous magnitude and significance of the commitments, the powerful sentiments that link us with prior generations since time immemorial, and the enduring and exclusive commitment to union while facing the uncertainties of life to come. The ritualism symbolically binds the families of the man and woman and attests to the importance of the unbreakable commitments of which God is both witness and participant.

12. What is the view of marriage as a contractual relationship? (313)

Marriage is viewed as a contractual relationship when it focuses on a mutually beneficial relationship and getting as opposed to giving. When the benefits stop flowing or hard times arise, the relationship is easily broken through divorce. The contract mentality in marriage emphasizes the details, e.g., "If you do that for me, I'll do this for you." In other words, the marital ledgers must always be balanced, but marriage partners often have differing views of the value of what is given and received. These differing perceptions in a marriage often result in growing resentment, hurt, anger, and ultimately divorce.

13. What is the view of marriage as a covenant relationship? (314)

Although a covenant marriage is also a contract, the similarity ends there. The covenant relationship is the essence of the cultural universal of marriage and is uniquely expressed in Christianity. Rather than to receive something in return, covenants are initiated for the benefit of others, that is, to minister to another person as opposed to manipulating someone to get something. In a covenant marriage, the *motive* is a commitment to the well-being of the spouse. In a covenant relationship, the promises made are not conditional but open-ended, that is, the promise or commitment is not conditioned on reciprocal behavior. There are no "If...then" clauses in covenant marriage vows.

14. How does the humanist worldview as described in *Humanist Manifesto II* conflict with the concept of covenant marriage? (314-315)

Two of the common principles of *Humanist Manifesto II* clearly elevate the individual as opposed to the two who shall become one flesh. Fifth Principle: "The preciousness and dignity of the *individual* person is a central humanist value...We reject all religious, ideological, or moral codes that denigrate the individual, suppress freedom, dull intellect, dehumanize personality." Sixth Principle: "In the area of sexuality, we believe that intolerant attitudes, often cultivated by orthodox religions and puritanical cultures, unduly repress sexual conduct. The right to birth control, abortion, and divorce should be recognized."

15. What are the fruits of the ascending humanist worldview since the 1960s with regard to marriage and family? (319)

In their flight from marriage, humanists promised women emancipation and fulfillment, but they received only bondage, drudgery, and exhaustion—poverty, long hours of daily separation from their children, and the drudgery of low-paying jobs in the workforce. The rise of the humanist worldview in America has born bitter fruit—illegitimacy, cohabitation, fatherlessness, divorce, and a large number of single parent families with children who are locked in a continuing cycle of neglect and poverty. When compared to homes where children were raised by married parents, children raised in homes by single parents are more likely to encounter emotional and behavioral problems, drink, smoke, use drugs, be physically abused, exhibit poor school performance and drop out, and exhibit aggressive, violent, and criminal behavior.

Chapter 21 – American Family – Feminism and the Roles of Men and Women

1. Describe Stephanie Coontz's role characterization of the male breadwinner/full-time housewife marriages. (323)

Coontz states that the once radical concept that love should be the basis for marriage and that the couple should control the decision process began in the late eighteenth century and continued to grow until the 1950s and 1960s in America and Western Europe. This concept was the basis for the male/female roles as male breadwinner and the female role of full-time housewife. The concept was embraced by both those with the Christian and humanist worldviews. However, the interpretation and implementation of the concept love-based and couple's choice concept was radically different in the two worldviews.

2. What was the general view of the roles of husbands and wives throughout history? (323)

Typically, men in all cultures and times have been the defenders of and providers for the family whereas women have been the nurturers and care givers for husband and children. Although those roles may not have finite and sharp distinctions (husbands and wives may share most roles in varying degrees), the basic defender-provider/nurturer-care giver dichotomy remains a constant. For much of history, marriage was not primarily about love. Rather, the needs and desires of the man and woman and their children were secondary to the needs of the larger group. Through marital status within the group came adulthood and respectability.

3. How and when did the roles of husband and wife emerge as society was transformed from a barter to a wage-based economy? (324)

In early barter economies wives were part of the family labor force with production centered in the home. Wives combined their productive tasks with that of motherhood and domestic chores. However, as societies moved from barter to wage-based economies, production occurred outside of the home, and it became more difficult for women to perform both roles. The new division of labor found the father and children working outside the home while wives concentrated on domestic activities which included traditional tasks and care of younger children but also growing food, cooking, home maintenance, making clothes, and tending to animals. With prosperity, women's roles became less a matter of economic survival but one of homemaking which was viewed as an act of love and a mark of a family's economic status and social success. From this transition developed the new role and identity of wives. Homemaking lost its status as an economic activity. Women were no longer considered work-mates—economic producers and co-providers—but soul mates.

4. How has the humanist worldview of marriage and sexuality undermined the traditional roles of men and women? (326)

In modern Western societies, strains to marital unions have grown significantly through demands of equality in marital relationships. The denigration of the traditional roles of husbands and wives has resulted in a general decline in the perceived importance and sanctity of the institution of marriage. Demands for equality are a direct attack on the hierarchical nature of the marriage relationship. This quest for equality in the marriage relationship is a caustic that will eat away at the coveted and sublime self-giving that occurs through unconditional commitment at all levels of the marital relationship.

5. How did the Industrial Revolution impact American society and ultimately the status of women? (327)

The Industrial Revolution in the first half of the nineteenth century brought significant changes to America in the form of urbanization, industrialization, and rapid social changes. It was from the beginning of Andrew Jackson's presidency to the beginning of the Civil War that significant attitudinal changes occurred with regard to slavery, health, prisons, education, social relationships, and the status of women. Between 1815 and 1860, two groups emerged to address the turmoil in society and bring order the souls of Americans. Out of the religious renewal and fervor arose a more democratic brand of Protestantism that tended toward perfectionism or a sin-free world in this life as opposed to the Puritan emphasis on the afterlife. The second group included hundreds of utopian communalist and transcendentalist societies bent on reordering social and economic systems while rejecting "…any social arrangements, tradition, church doctrine, or even familial relationships as expressions of power. Marriage, they held, constituted just another form of oppression, even slavery…"

6. With regard to the status of women, what was the agenda for the utopians and religious perfectionists and how was it to be achieved? (327)

Many utopians and religious perfectionists supported greater rights and roles for women. These included property rights, divorce, child custody, education, and greater opportunities and roles in the work place; although, not all groups supported all of these rights. Women increasingly saw political means as a way to solve personal problems.

7. How did Margaret Sanger package her goals of radical socialism and sexual liberation so that it would be readily accepted in the United States? (330-331)

She founded the Birth Control League, and began publication of *The Birth Control Review*. Her stature rose among the urban intelligentsia and subscriptions soared as she solicited articles from well-known authors such as H. G. Wells, Julian Huxley, and Karl Menninger for her *Birth Control Review*. Her widespread fame grew with the publication in 1922 of her book *The Pivot of Civilization*.

8. As Nazi atrocities became known during World War II, how did Sanger overcome her close association with German scientists who designed Nazi Germany's "race purification" plan; her endorsement of early Reich euthanasia, sterilization, abortion, and infanticide programs; and the articles in her *Birth Control Review* that closely paralleled Nazi Aryan-White Supremacist propaganda? (331)

Margaret embarked on a three-pronged program to rescue herself and her organization from its infamous connection with Nazi Germany and its massacres: change the name of her organization to Planned Parenthood Federation of America, found a national birth control organization under which local and regional birth control leagues would affiliate and contribute their grassroots respectability, and initiate a massive propaganda campaign to emphasize patriotism and family values while hiding her scandalous personal life and political views.

9. How did Betty Friedan and other feminists of the early 1960s and 1970s hope to change society with regard to women and families (as described in the National Organization of Women's Statement of Purpose)? (333-334)

Friedan called upon Boomers and their daughters to embrace "...the family in new terms of equality and diversity..." with emphasis on *redesigning* the family structure. For the feminists of the 1960s and 70s, conventional marriage and family were at best an option for a few, but they questioned its allure in a "progressive" society in which "marriage and children limited women's career success and prevented them from the adventure and self-exploration that seemed men's privilege."

10. Regarding marriage, what have been the consequences to America as the humanist philosophy of feminists (e.g., Betty Friedan) has been embraced by large portions of society? (334)

America is experiencing the wreckage, misery, and unhappiness of divorce, cohabitation, out-of-wedlock births, poverty, and single family households. From these consequences humanists and feminists discovered the inflexibility of human universals such as marriage.

11. Why is the Judeo-Christian worldview with regard to marriage superior to the humanist worldview of the feminists of the 1960s and 1970s? (334)

Extensive research has revealed marriage was good for men and women and that a gender balance rather than gender bias existed within marriage. The benefits of marriage for *both* men and women include greater happiness and satisfaction in life, greater combined financial success, greater sexual satisfaction, better psychological and physical health, and less exposure to physical violence.

12. Why is marriage central to the overall well-being of children and why is the humanistic worldview so destructive to that well-being? (336)

The primary duty of parents is to socialized their children, i.e., to imbue within those children the central vision of society that is consistent with the central and accepted truths of human history. It is through marriage and family in the home that such socialization occurs and by which society achieves order and continuation. The rapid rise of the humanistic worldview beginning in the 1960s put forth monumental challenges to the transmission of the moral order upon which American society had flourished. Those challenges include illegitimacy, cohabitation, fatherlessness, homosexual lifestyle, and divorce. It is those things that erode the foundation of marriage, family, and home and effectively cast children on a rootless quest for meaning in life.

13. According to Waite and Gallaher, what gives marriage and family centrality and power within the universal social institutions? (338)

"As a species, we have developed social institutions over eons to get the most out of these creatures that we are. The family, focused around the married couple, forms the keystone of these universal social institutions." And the foundation of the married couple is at its strongest when bound with those simple non-conditional commitments to "…love and cherish, till death do us part."

Chapter 22 – American Family – Abortion

1. Why is it that the contrary understanding of life and its origin are at the root of the division between humanist and Christian worldviews? (341-342)

For those with Judeo-Christian beliefs, God is the creator of the universe and all within including man, and consequently God and His universal laws are the arbiters of the life and death of men and no one else. For the humanist, life and its origins have nothing to do with God. Humanists have devalued God, and "When man devalues God, he eventually comes to devalue man, as well as the animating factor we call life." Because of this fundamental difference, it is understandable that the most contentious and emotional issue of our times in the war between humanist and Christian worldviews revolves around abortion of unborn babies.

2. How did the rise of Christianity create a basic change in the world with regard to unborn and infant children? (342-343)

For all of ancient history few voices were raised against the wanton slaughter of children. It was the dramatic and rapid spread of Christianity in the second and third centuries throughout the Mediterranean world that propelled the new and novel notion that life was sacred. However, it was not the newness or novelty of the idea that captured the civilized world and achieved a cultural consensus. The power in the message of the sanctity of life came from the Scriptural revelation and the universal affirmation and action of the church world. The message that abortion and infanticide were murder rang loudly and clearly from the foundation of Christianity and for nineteen centuries thereafter. Not only did the Church affirm and proclaim its message, the most profound impact on the civilized world came as a result of the Church *living* its message.

3. How do humanists separate the decisions of life from God? (343-344)

Humanist Manifesto II states "that moral values derive their source from human experience. Ethics is autonomous and situational, needing no theological or ideological sanction…" For the humanist, decisions of life depend on the current situation, human experience, needs of the moment, and interests of society.

4. How do humanists soften the picture or divert attention from the horror of abortion? (344)

Through use of euphemisms, platitudes, and legal arguments about rights, privacy, and choice.

5. Upon what legal arguments did the Supreme Court's majority opinion rely in the Roe v. Wade decision to allow abortion? (347)

The majority believed that although the Constitution does not explicitly mention any right of privacy, the Fourteenth Amendment's concept of personal liberty and restrictions upon state action and the Ninth Amendment's reservation of rights to the people were "…broad enough to encompass a woman's decision whether or not to terminate her pregnancy."

6. How did the Supreme Court's majority opinion respond to the contention of those opposed to abortion that "life begins at conception and is present throughout pregnancy…" and what is the fallacy of the court's majority opinion? (347-348)

The majority opinion stated that the court need not resolve the difficult question of when life begins. It argued that when those trained in the respective disciplines of medicine, philosophy, and theology are unable to arrive at any consensus, the judiciary at this point in the development of man's knowledge, is not in a position to speculate as to the answer. The fallacy of the majority's opinion that it need not resolve the question of when life begins is found in its own statements. On the one hand the court says it need not resolve the question while on the other hand it admits that if life began at conception the case for the proponents of abortion would fail, that is, if the fetus attained personhood, then the fetus' right to life would be guaranteed specifically by the Fourteenth Amendment.

7. How do abortionists' arguments that life does not begin until birth fail? (348-349)

The case for abortion is exceptionally weak in both fields of logic and science. One of the first arguments submitted by those supporting legalized abortion was an attempt to separate the existence of a human in the moral sense from the existence of a human being in the biological sense. For abortionists, human beings exist in a moral sense and have rights at the point of consciousness. From the biological perspective, the pre-conscious human beings exist but do not have rights. Thus, pro-abortion proponents arbitrarily pin existence to consciousness. From scientific and logical standpoints, the abortionists' problem of defending abortion is compounded. To affix consciousness to the occurrence of some physical event other than the beginning of the continuum of life is wholly arbitrary. The line between the zygote and adult human being is continuous, that is, there are no "biological interruptions, or gaps" from embryo to adult. Being a distinct, self-integrating organism is the issue, not dependence on the mother (before or after birth). By any reasonable measure, the weight of pro-life arguments prevails and the abortionists' arguments fail in both realms of science and logic.

8. What has been the effect of the Supreme Court's 1973 Roe v. Wade legalization of abortion decision on other life issues? (350-351)

Abortion was merely "...the wedge used to split open the historic Western commitment to the dignity of human life." Once unleashed, abortion coarsened society with regard to the sanctity of life. The issue of abortion quickly moved from a woman's right of privacy to a tool of public policy. The humanists' coveted right of choice moved across the line from abortion to infanticide in the 1982 case of "Baby Doe." Many scientists and academics would not stop at "allowing" children to die. Some such as Francis Crick support screening newborns, and those that fail to meet certain health standards would be euthanized. Peter Singer believes that parents ought to be allowed to kill their disabled children. His reasoning is "...that they are 'nonpersons' until they are rational and self-conscious." Singer extends his reasoning to the "...killing of incompetent persons of any age if their families decide their lives are 'not worth living'." The progression of the humanists' assault on life was inevitable once life was separated from God: the abortion of unborn children, infanticide, and euthanasia of persons of any age who are disabled, non-rational, lacking self-consciousness, or generally judged as having lives "not worth living."

Chapter 23 – American Family – Homosexuality

1. What is the biblical position with regard to homosexuality?

The Genesis account reveals God's abhorrence of homosexuality as demonstrated by the destruction of Sodom. Probably the most important statement reflecting the Judeo-Christian view of homosexuality is given in the New Testament book of Romans (1:18-32) and specifically in verses 24-27. (353)

> Therefore God gave them up in the lusts of their hearts to impurity, to the dishonoring of their bodies among themselves, because they exchanged the truth about God for a lie and worshiped and served the creature rather than the Creator, who is blessed for ever! For this reason God gave them up to dishonorable passions. Their women exchanged natural relations for unnatural, and the men likewise gave up natural relations with women and were consumed with passion for one another, men committing shameless acts with men and receiving in their own persons the due penalty of their error." [Romans 1:24-27 RSV.]

2. What impact does homosexuality have on society, and how do those that support homosexuality diminish marriage and the elevate homosexuality? (354)

Humans have fashioned numerous methods by which to organize their societies, but the common link to all is the family unit—a father, a mother, and children living together in bonds of committed caring. It is the fundamental unit upon which societies are built. By contrast, homosexuality is a disorganizing concept with regard to human relationships and ultimately disorganizing in building stable, enduring societies. Proponents wish to lift the status of homosexuality in society through its attainment of legitimacy, legal identity, and respect as a cultural tradition, that is, a place at the table so to speak. These efforts involve court challenges to long-standing and culturally established norms, enactment of laws which favor the homosexual agenda and that diminish marriage, and promotion of homosexuality in the popular culture.

3. What are the two general conceptions of marriage in society, and which is supported by the proponents of homosexuality? (354-355)

The Judeo-Christian concept is that marriage and children born of that marriage is at the core of society and by default is limited to heterosexual marriage relationships. The humanist concept of marriage is that it is essentially a private relationship, and from this concept comes the attack by the proponents of the homosexual agenda. The legislative and legal efforts to redefine marriage to include homosexual couples of either gender, whether in law or culture, weaken the idea of a mother and father for every child. Marriage, under the homosexual definition, is "…a loving, self-determining couple engaging in an ordinary civil contract that has nothing to do with children." Under the homosexual definition of marriage, children are not central to the relationship.

4. What is the humanist's argument that homosexuals should be allowed to marry? (355)

Humanists deny that marriage is inherently heterosexual. As such reasoning goes, the value of sex derives from *either* procreation *or* pleasure. It would then follow that the motivation for heterosexual acts and homosexual acts may be similar for reasons other than procreation. Therefore, there is a bias in traditional matrimonial laws which unfairly penalize homosexuals by preventing them from attaining status through marriage.

5. What is the Judeo-Christian worldview's answer to the humanist with regard homosexuals being allowed to marry? (355-356)

Within a heterosexual marriage, pleasure in sexual union is rightly sought and perfects the marital union. However, in the traditional view of marriage, the value of sex is *intrinsic*, not merely to attain pleasure or some other extrinsic value. The principal intrinsic value and purpose of sexual union "…is *marriage itself*, considered as a bodily (one-flesh) union of persons consummated and actualized by acts that are reproductive in type." Why only *reproductive* acts? The heterosexual marriage relationship is "naturally ordered to the good of procreation (and to the nurturing and education of children)." The strength and depth of spousal commitment and unity that derives from a marriage consummated by the reproductive act, whether intended for purposes of procreation or not, cannot be matched by any other relationship. The nature of the reproductive acts in marriage are distinctly and intrinsically unitive and achieves a meshing of persons that transcends the instrumental or extrinsic purposes of the act itself.

6. How do proponents of the homosexual agenda attempt to gain the moral high ground with their arguments? (356-357)

To oppose homosexuality is deemed the moral equivalence of racism, bigotry, ignorance, and homophobia. Those persons who are not accepting of homosexuality are labeled as intolerant. For those that fail to enter the humanist shrine of tolerance, they become the objects of intolerant harassment through restrictions on free speech (speech codes), coercion, and intimidation. To the proponents of homosexuality, tolerance means forced acceptance, and such acceptance necessitates "normalization, validation, public legitimation, and finally public endorsement."

7. With regard the humanist/homosexual agenda of normalization, validation, legitimation, and endorsement, what is the answer from the Judeo-Christian worldview? (357)

Traditional marriage between a man and a woman is the standard (universal). Homosexuality is a significant and fatal deviation from that standard and does not warrant normalization, validation, public legitimation, or public endorsement in the central vision of culture in America.

8. Then what should be the attitude be toward the homosexual if one holds the Judeo-Christian worldview? (357)

If God loves and respects the homosexual as an individual member of the creation, so should those that disagree with the homosexual's actions. That means those holding the Judeo-Christian worldview should treat homosexuals with respect and fairness that is due any other human being. However, like God, we do not accept or approve their actions. Nor should society allow the homosexual practices to be

101

normalized, validated, endorsed, or given any form of legitimacy such as allowing same-sex marriages or homosexual adoptions.

9. How have the proponents of homosexuality used the judicial system to further their agenda? (358)

Under the guise of discrimination, proponents of the homosexual agenda use court challenges to strike down laws that are supposedly the result of bigotry and prejudice. The practical effect of rulings of unconstitutionality since the middle of the twentieth century is that the successful challenges to laws that maintain the mores and traditions upon which the nation was founded become the basis for policy initiatives of the "cultural elite on the far left of the American political spectrum." These rulings result in policy initiatives that are humanistic in origin and spread throughout the various American institutions as judicially blessed laws, policies, directives, rules, and regulations of the land.

10. Why have many mainstream Christian churches linked themselves to the humanistic worldview with regard to their affinity for the cause of homosexuality? (360)

Tocqueville warned that "…when religion aims to depend upon the principles of this world, it becomes almost as vulnerable as all other powers on this earth. By itself, it may aspire to immortality but, linked to fleeting powers, it follows their fortunes and often collapses together with those passions which sustain them for a day." Tocqueville's words were prophetic for those churches that support homosexuality and its agenda have seen their number of adherents decline dramatically.

11. How does one holding the Judeo-Christian worldview answer proponents of homosexuality who cite various scientific studies that indicate sexual orientation is a matter of genetics, i.e., sexual orientation is involuntary, immutable, and rooted in nature"? (361)

First we must address the belief that sexual orientation is a matter of genetics. There are no reliable studies that indicate a genetic link to homosexuality, that is, a genetic causation. In studies that have indicated otherwise, the supposed link is so small or weak as to be inconsequential. Others surrender on the issue of genetic *causation* but continue to hold to genetic *predisposition* to homosexuality. Here we move the second part of the argument in support of homosexuality: If homosexuality was found to have a genetic basis, then moral distinctions are invalid as it relates to differences between homosexuality and heterosexuality. But this too is an invalid argument for neither genetic causation nor predisposition justifies cultural acceptance. Should such genetic links exist, they do not justify immoral behavior whether it is alcoholism, criminal activities, or homosexuality. People are not slaves to their passions, desires, and predispositions as humanists would have us believe. Some people will struggle with those forces more than others, but people have the ability to choose their behavior.

Chapter 24 – Popular Culture

1. What is popular culture and its connection to a society's central cultural vision? (367)

By popular (contemporary) culture is meant the well-known and generally accepted cultural patterns or lifestyles that are widespread within a culture. Generally, popular culture is a reflection of a society's core values or central cultural vision. The popular culture may change over time but still be supportive of the central cultural vision. However, disintegration of any society will be accelerated by a popular culture that is at odds with the central cultural vision. Unrestrained by tradition or other moral force, popular culture can lead to rebellion against the cultural central vision of a society. Tradition, by itself, can only maintain a central cultural vision for a time as the moral capital upon which the vision was built is eroded. Popular culture that misreads or wars against the validity of a morally sound central cultural vision will either be destroyed or cause that society, to which popular culture stands in opposition, to disintegrate.

2. How is popular culture shaped and what are the two greatest forces that influence popular culture? (367-368)

Popular culture is not so much an institution of American life but rather a reflection of the combined faces of its institutions that shape popular culture. Nevertheless, as popular culture is being shaped by other forces, it attains a critical mass and power to shape or bend society's central cultural vision. Two of the greatest forces influencing popular culture are the arts and mass media.

3. What is the classical understanding of the purpose of art? (368)

In the classical understanding, the purpose of the arts was to represent something significant about reality and truth and thereby guide, enrich, and sustain culture. This was objectivism by which is meant belief in objective reality and in which moral good is objectively real. This reality is not one of static or restrictive repetition but of amplification, clarification, and inspiration. Through the classical view of art we may see God rooted in the structure, orderliness, and harmony of His creation and its universals, and the classical view can be presented

104

through various art forms such as painting, architecture, literature, dance, theater, and music.

4. How was the classical view of art undermined? (368-369)

According to Kirk, "Every major form of literary art has taken for its deeper themes the norms of human nature…'the permanent things'…to teach human beings their true nature, their dignity, and their place in the scheme of things." As the eighteenth century came to a close and the religious view of life began to decay, this normative purpose of literature was replaced by "…the literature of nihilism, of pornography and of sensationalism…" The undermining of the authority of religion and the purpose of art through the influences of the Renaissance and Enlightenment had devastating effects by the end of the eighteenth century. The assault on the religious view of life and art continued in the nineteenth century as science became the sole source of knowledge. For the rationalists, art was a "falsification of reality" or "at best "merely an expression of personal emotion" rather than a means to represent something significant about reality and truth.

5. Describe the humanistic influence on art and how it captured the arts from the classical view. (369-370)

The humanistic influence on the arts is called subjectivism (as opposed to Judeo-Christian objectivism). At the heart of subjectivism there are no standards of right or wrong, good or bad, and moral or immoral. Concepts of quality become irrelevant as the humanistic tenet of equality dictates that the art of the struggling beginner is just as good as the work of an accomplished artist with a lifetime of experience. The humanists' capture of the arts from the classical view was accomplished through the exaltation of the individual, "…a view of the individual person which gives unprecedented weight to his or her choices, interests, and claims."

6. Summarize the differences between the humanistic and Christian worldviews with regard to the arts. (370)

For the humanist, the arts are experiential, temporal, and valueless and whose appeal is based on its ability to stimulate the senses, to entertain, and to shock, all of which are inherently individualistic and therefore fragmentary to culture. For the Christian, the arts are meant to reflect the *reality* of God's glory, beauty, and truth, and through such we enhance our moral and spiritual development and understanding, all of which are inherently unifying to culture.

7. What is the relationship between mass media and popular culture, and to which worldview does mass media have a tendency to lean towards (humanistic or Judeo-Christian)? (370)

Mass media and popular culture demonstrate a symbiotic relationship. Each feeds off of as well as reflects the other. Modern mass media, particularly the electronic variety, is an inherently humanistic and secularizing force in popular culture.

8. What is the first source of the secular and humanistic tendencies of mass media? Briefly describe. (373)

The first source is the structural nature of mass media. This structure results in the *loss of linkage with reality*. Malcolm Muggeridge contends that "modern mass media—and particularly television— insulate us from the reality of the moral order...the media have created, and belong to, a world of fantasy, the more dangerous because it purports to be, and is largely taken as being, the real world." The structure of the media tends toward *superficiality* and focuses on the *immediacy* of events which creates a disconnection between time and eternity. Fact driven reporting trounces understanding, and information overwhelms wisdom. Mass media is also *leveling or relativistic* by which is meant that trivial events of the moment receive attention beyond their importance. By doing so, journalism makes all things of relatively equal importance and thereby diminishes concepts of cultural and eternal importance.

9. What the second source of the secular and humanistic tendencies of mass media? Briefly describe. (374)

The second source of mass media's secular and humanistic influence on popular culture is the overwhelmingly predominant secular and humanistic worldview of the individuals and institutions controlling mass media. Rather than reinforcing those principles, morals, and manners, modern mass media molds public opinion by setting the agenda and influencing what people think about. This has led to a cultural shift as the mass media's humanistic worldview has ascended while the Christian worldview is marginalized and demeaned through substantial and constant attack.

10. What are the three components of mass media? (375)

The three components are informational-political, popular entertainment, and advertising.

11. What was Robert Bork's assessment of popular entertainment in America? (375)

"In keeping with the progress of liberalism, popular entertainment generally—and the worst of it in particular— celebrates the unconstrained self, and savages those who would constrain."

12. How does advertising promote the humanistic worldview in popular culture? (376)

Although a legitimate and often necessary form of communication, advertising is often a willing accomplice in the propagation of the humanistic worldview as it is driven by the winds of popular culture. However, advertising is not just a pawn reflecting the desires of popular culture, it also influences it. And much of the secular, humanistic influence of advertising is aimed at children and young people.

13. How does the flood of information available in modern society undermine the Judeo-Christian worldview? (378)

The source of this flood is the secularizing mass media which dictates the cultural agenda and what people think about. Its broad channels of dissemination are information (news, politics, and minutia of popular culture), entertainment, and advertising. This flood of information hinders thoughtfulness and ultimately our understanding without which formless chaos reigns. In the torrents of chaos, if we are not diligent, we lose sight of our Judeo-Christian culture's central vision and perish.

14. What is the first of two means whereby secular humanists attempt explain and defend popular culture from being a source of the decay in America life and what is the response from someone holding the Judeo-Christian worldview? (380)

On the one hand, liberals submit that such is the "price you pay for freedom of expression." However, when the humanistic ideal of unrestrained freedom of expression is more important that the quality of American life, something is amiss with that worldview.

15. What is the second of two means whereby secular humanists attempt explain and defend popular culture from being a source of the decay in American life and what is the response from someone holding the Judeo-Christian worldview? (380-381)

The second defense is that the root causes of crime and violence do not lay with popular culture. Karen Sternheimer believes that, "The roots of the most serious problems American children face, problems like lack of a quality education, violent victimization, early pregnancies, single parenthood, and obesity, poverty plays a starring role; popular culture is a bit player at best." Rather than blame mass media, it "…can be used to redirect our attention to the sources of our society's problems and to provide us with a wake-up call about the persistence of inequality in the United States." Again, we see the humanistic call for equality that has been discussed extensively in this book and which has been shown to not be the solution to "…education, violence, teen pregnancy, family instability, health, substance use, sexism, racism, and homophobia…" as humanists would have us believe.

Part IV – Ye shall be as gods – Summary, Status, and Direction

Chapter 25 – Differences between Christian and Humanist Worldviews – A Summary

1. What is this book about? (385)

This book is about a clash of Christian and humanistic worldviews, principally in modern America. The origins of the opposing views and their impact on the major institutions of American have been documented and discussed throughout this book.

2. What is the difference in the Christian and humanist worldviews with regard to God and creation? (385)

In the Christian worldview, God existed before time, creation of the universe, and all therein including the earth and mankind. He stood outside the universe and created matter out of nothing. Humanism denies the existence of a supernatural, creative force in the creation of the universe. Its gospel is naturalism which insists that the unending universe of space and time are all parts of one great Nature including the earth and human beings.

3. What is the difference in the Christian and humanist worldviews with regard to man's purpose? (386)

God created mankind for a special and mutual relationship with the Creator. Man's purpose is to glorify God, to love and be loved by Him, and to enjoy interacting with Him and His creation for eternity. In the humanist worldview, the main purpose of human life is to advance the happiness of man through the development, enjoyment, and making available to all the abundant material, cultural and spiritual goods of this natural world.

4. What is the difference in the Christian and humanist worldviews with regard to man's creation and free will? (386)

In the Christian worldview, man was the noblest of God's creatures and singly endowed with reason and free will. Man through his free will was allowed to choose or not choose to constrain his actions and conform to and be in obedience to the Creator's laws of human nature. Therefore, man can and will be held accountable for right and wrong behaviors. In the humanist worldview, man and his human nature were not created by a Supreme Being but are products of evolution. Man is merely a complex animal without notions of moral responsibility. Humans and other life forms are the products of an infinitely long process of evolution that exceeds three billion years.

5. What is the difference in the Christian and humanist worldviews with regard to man's nature? (387)

In the Christian worldview, man is a fallen creature. Mankind's free will allowed man to think and act in ways that were contrary to God's plan and will for His creation. When man acted in ways contrary to God's laws (truths), such disobedience was called sin, and as a result decay and death entered into God's creation. For the humanist, man is continuously perfectible, a process whereby he will become progressively better and better. Man is not fallen and does not need redemption.

6. What is the difference in the Christian and humanist worldviews with regard to man's position and destiny? (387-388)

Unregenerate man is positionally separated from God because of man's inherited sinful nature. The Christian worldview holds that man is inherently fallen because of the entry of sin in to the human race (original sin) and therefore is separated from God. Through His son, Jesus Christ, God allows man through an act of his free will to get out of the mess he created. For man who rejects God's son through his free choice, the gulf separating him from God remains un-crossable, and the emptiness and pain caused by his broken relationship and separation from his creator will torment his being for eternity. In the humanist worldview, man is the evolutionary product of Nature, and his mind is inextricably joined with the functioning of his brain. There is no conscious survival after death because of the unity of body and personality (which includes every aspect of the mind).

7.   What is the difference in the Christian and humanist
     worldviews with regard to man's relationship to man? (389)

In the Christian worldview, man is made for relationship which implies
dwelling together. It is one of the fundamental needs of mankind. Man
was made in the image of God, and the importance of human
relationships is a reflection of the Trinitarian relationship. The
humanist views man's relationship with man through the distorted lens
of equality. The distortion arises as equality goes beyond equality of
man before God (which humanism denies) and the law. It is also an
equality that goes beyond equality of opportunity to equality of
outcome.

8.   What is the difference in the Christian and humanist
     worldviews with regard to man as an individual? (389)

The Christian believes that each individual was created for a personal
and loving relationship with God, but that relationship was broken with
all of mankind when man sinned. Therefore, a personal (individual)
relationship with God is possible only through recognition of who God
is and obedience to his precepts. The broken relationship is restored by
the individual through the acceptance of God's son, Jesus Christ, as his
Lord and Savior. Humanists hold that the preciousness and dignity of
the individual person is a central humanist value in which individuals
should be encouraged to realize their own creative talents and desires
and exercise maximum individual autonomy consonant with social
responsibility.

9.   What is the difference in the Christian and humanist
     worldviews with regard to societal organization and
     governments? (389-390)

In the Christian worldview, sustained order in society is possible only
when its citizens achieve order of their individual souls within God's
laws. As a man orders his individual soul in accordance with God's
timeless truths, he also contributes to an orderly society that promotes
harmonious relationships with nature and between individuals within
that society. Society contains many elements of which government is
only one. The Christian worldview sees governments as ordained by

God for its own distinctive civil purposes and not for church purposes. The Church and government are separate institutions, but that does not imply a wall of separation stands between them. Humanists link organization of society to the enhancement of freedom and dignity of the individual which occurs when a "full range of individual liberties" is experienced. For the humanist, government must ultimately and inevitably assume a socialistic form in order to deliver the promised human satisfactions and eradication of disproportionate wealth, income, and economic growth.

10. What is the difference between the Christian and humanist worldviews with regard to religion? (390-391)

The Christian believes that religion is man's feeble efforts to cross the gulf between fallen man and God. It is endemic to all of mankind, in every age and every people group. However, apart from the truth offered by the Judeo-Christian ethic, religion remains powerless to span the gulf that was created by sin. In the humanist worldview, religion is a human social construction. Its presence merely occurs as means to draw people together and give meaning to their lives. There is no room for supernaturalism for religion is merely a form of human experience and values. Human justice, not a dead God, gives meaning to those human experiences and values.

11. What is the difference between the Christian and humanist worldviews with regard to marriage and family? (391)

The supreme reflection of God's image in humankind is in the marriage relationship followed by family. The roles of husband and wife and father and mother (monogamous married couple living with their children) are not societal constructs. The divinely ordered family *structure* is intrinsically a part of the fundamental identity of the family in every society and for all time. It is one of those universals or permanent things imbedded in the foundation of creation. The humanistic worldview and its values focus on the individual person and his/her independence, freedom, self-actualization, autonomy, growth, and creativity. Marriage is not central or necessary for nurturing and the transmission of moral and cultural values to children. The pair-bonding elements of monogamy and permanency are individual decisions and not cultural universals.

12. What means have humanists used to dislodge the Judeo-Christian worldview as the central vision of American culture? (392)

Richard Weaver believes that this has been accomplished by an attack on language. In our modern age humanists have effectively used semantics to neuter words of their meaning in historical and symbolic contexts, that is, words now mean what men want them to mean. By removing the fixities of language (which undermines an understanding of truth), language loses its ability to define and compel. As the meaning of words is divorced from truth, relativism gains supremacy, and a culture tends to disintegration without an understanding of eternal truths upon which to orient its self.

13. What is the difference in Christian and humanist worldviews with regard to the meaning of truth? (392-393)

In the Christian worldview, the Supreme Being (God) formed the universe and God created matter out of nothing. He impressed certain principles upon that matter, from which it can never depart, and without which it would cease to be. Those principles are truths that are intrinsic, timeless, and are essential elements that provide a coherent and rational way to live in the world. These absolutes are called by various names: permanent things, universals, first principles, eternal truths, and norms. The humanistic worldview regarding truth is one of cultural relativism which requires a suspension of judgment since all belief systems contain some truth within while no one belief system has all the truth. For humanists, all social constructions are culturally relative as they are shaped by class, gender, and ethnicity. Thus, there can be no universal truths because all viewpoints, lifestyles, and beliefs are equally valid. No man or group can claim to be infallible with regard to truth and virtue.

14. What is the difference between the Christian and humanist worldviews with regard to the meaning of freedom? (393)

Simply put, freedom means an absence of coercion and constraint, but freedom does not mean an absence of consequences. God created man with a free will, that is, God gave man a choice as to whether to follow or not follow God's laws and commandments. Freedom, under the humanists' perverted definition, unbridled the self and senses from any control except within the strictures imposed by the greater good for humanity. The humanist definition of freedom presumes to loose man from the bondage of mores, norms, tradition, and distant voices of the past. However, the humanists' definition of freedom, which co-joins the maximization of individual autonomy with the humanist-created primacy of the greatest good for the greatest number, is a false freedom.

15. What is the difference between the Christian and humanist worldviews with regard to the meaning of democracy? (394)

Democracy is a form of government by the people, rule of the majority, and a means of voting. Democracy is not a synonym for freedom. Humanists have appropriated, redefined the term, and have used it to arbitrarily consolidate power and limit individual freedom. The humanist definition of democracy has been infused with moral principles such as a commitment to liberty and equality, concern for the worth and dignity of the individual, an individual's right to do what he wishes and limits undue interference with his individual choice and action, opportunity for growth and personal realization, tolerance, and diversity. Each carries with it its own humanistic meaning. For humanists, democracy is both method *and* goal, a means *and* an end. In effect, democracy has been elevated to something of value in itself.

16. What is the difference between the Christian and humanist worldviews with regard to the meaning of equality? (395)

Here we speak of equality of the individual. The founding Americans relied on order that rested upon a respect for prescriptive rights and customs as opposed to the egalitarian notions of the French philosophers during the French Revolution. For the Founders who held the Judeo-Christian worldview, equality meant equality before God and before the law. The humanists' concept of human equality flows from the humanistic assumption of the perfectibility of man. As men are equal at birth, differences and inequalities arise due to environment. The goal of humanists was to achieve an egalitarian society through political means which meant equality of condition. When humanists failed to achieve equality of outcome through political means, the levelers demanded economic democracy, a new and expanded humanist definition of equality, but it still means an equality of condition as opposed to equality of opportunity and is to be achieved through recognition of invented or synthetic rights coupled with broad but non-specific egalitarian ideals.

17. What is the difference in the Christian and humanist worldviews with regard to the meaning of justice? (396)

Justice is variously defined as fairness, impartiality, right action, and the principle or process by which every man and woman in society are accorded the things that inherently belong to them (their lives, dignity, property, and status or station in life). The concept of justice is a universal, a thing of permanence that transcends the whole of man's time on this planet and pertains to all cultures. For the humanist, man is an economic being, and the definition of justice must be bent to recognized humanist social values. Those values—liberty and opportunity, income and wealth, and the bases of self-respect—are to be distributed equally unless an unequal distribution of any or all of these values is equally advantageous to everyone. These values, and therefore justice charged with upholding these values, are a thing rationally constructed by man.

18. What is the difference between the Christian and humanist worldviews with regard to the meaning of multiculturalism? (396-397)

The Judeo-Christian ethic recognizes the common origin of man as described in Genesis of the Old Testament. Christians understand that God created all peoples, but those peoples have developed different cultures and worldviews. Christianity far exceeds humanism and most other worldviews in its adaptation to and civil respect for diverse cultures and governments. Humanistic multiculturalism is defined as a belief that all cultures are equally valid and valuable, and it claims that all cultures offer some truth while no one culture can claim to provide the answers to all of life's basic questions. The essence of multiculturalism is found in the denial of absolutes, one of the cardinal tenets of the humanistic faith. Without absolutes, societies descend to moral relativism, a values-free approach that makes it impossible to judge one period or era in relation to another or to say that one culture's ethic is superior to another.

19. What is the difference between the Christian and humanist worldviews with regard to the meaning of diversity? (397-398)

The Christian's focus is not on the individual's differences but upon diversity's contribution to the whole of society, and from this emphasis comes unity. Unity is made possible when each member is recognized as an indispensable contributor to the body. Humanism's diversity is a close kin of multiculturalism and focuses on the differences within society and not society as a whole. With emphasis on the differences, mass culture becomes nothing more than an escalating number of subcultures within an increasingly distressed political framework that attempts to satisfy the myriad of demands of the individual subcultures. There is a loss of unity through fragmentation.

20. What is the difference between the Christian and humanist worldviews with regard to the meaning of tolerance? (398)

Regarding tolerance, Christian teaching speaks unerringly in defense of the concept of universal human rights and why each is obligated to respect the rights of others. The Christian's conflict with the humanist worldview regarding toleration arises with the humanist belief that man is a social animal, and his morality results from his innate altruism, a moral instinct of selflessness, though not equally developed in all humans. For the humanist, the origin of man's morality evolved from his ability to connect value or benefit with behaving well toward others, but that value does not originate with the laws established by a supernatural God.

21. What is the difference between the Christian and humanist worldviews with regard to the meaning of pluralism? (399)

A pluralistic society is one "…in which members of diverse ethnic, racial, religious, or social groups maintain an *autonomous participation* in and development of their traditional culture or special interest *within the confines of a common civilization*." By its very essence, culture must discriminate against those outside its boundaries that do not share its central vision. For the secular humanist, pluralism demands all religion be removed from the public square. This is a different interpretation of pluralism than held by Americans of the Revolutionary era. Pluralism in modern America, as defined by humanists, must presuppose that there are no universals, i.e., no God, and that all cultures are equally worthy and valid. It is in this humanistic definition of pluralism that cultures are prone to failure.

Chapter 26 – Christianity and Humanism – Endgame in America

1. How do cultures arise as a result of man seeing himself as a special being? (401-402)

Man senses his specialness, looks at himself and sees faint images of something far greater, and is compelled to search for answers as to the meaning and purpose of his life. Unique to the earth and its living creatures, man thinks, verbalizes, and symbolizes his quest for connection to some greater purpose. These yearnings become the felt needs of the group and represent an ordering of life in the larger sense—how things fit together and work and man's place in the grand scheme of things. This ordering is a process whereby the group determines what is true and right and a rejection of the way things are that are contrary to order. Out of the ordering process comes unity from which arises culture—the central vision of the group.

2. According to Richard Weaver, what are the elements that a culture requires? (402)

A culture must: recognize and believe in its uniqueness and worth; have a pattern of inclusion and exclusion, be inward facing toward some high representation, and be discriminating (determining what counts for much and what counts for little).

3. What were the colonists' and Founders' sources upon which they relied in creating the American central cultural vision upon which the nation was founded? (402)

The source of the American central cultural vision was drawn largely from the Judeo-Christian tradition and its reliance on a transcendent God, His eternal truths, and His revelation to the Hebrews and first century Christians. To these central elements were added the proscriptions of history, custom, convention, and tradition—in essence, our patrimony.

4. What was one of the Founders' greatest concerns when creating a government and how did they address their concerns? (403)

The Founders knew of the fallen nature of man and foresaw a time when men would attempt to change that which they had built on timeless truths. In their great wisdom, the Founders believed they should insure the government they built would not be changed capriciously by its inhabitants. So they devised the Constitution that limited those changes so the nation would continue to function within time-tested guidelines, or as Thomas Jefferson said, to "...bind him down with the chains of the Constitution."

5. According to the author, what are some of the time-tested truths within the American central cultural vision that humanists attempt to destroy and by what means? (403)

Some of the eternal truths are: belief in a transcendent God, hierarchy, moral truths, right and wrong, the fallen nature of man, and the sanctity of life. Because of the wisdom of the Founders in writing the Constitution, the humanists were slowed in their efforts to change the central cultural vision of the nation. So the progressives took the Founders' words and invented new definitions and meanings to attach to those words. Once the new meanings were defined by the humanist intellectual, taught in schools, and embedded in our media-saturated consciousness, the humanists insisted that the Constitution was outdated and must be modified and modernized to fit the new progressive understanding of the world and its problems.

6. How does the author distinguish between the permanence of the Judeo-Christian worldview and the endangered American cultural vision of the colonists and Founders? (404)

The Judeo-Christian worldview points to the ultimate truth, and that truth existed before the creation of this world and will exist after this world should God so choose to allow its demise. Cultures may disintegrate, but the truth of Christianity will not for it resides in the individual hearts of men and women. Christianity is not dependent on government sanction, and it does not have a political agenda apart from adherence to biblical principles. The truth of Christianity's lack of dependence on government sanction and absence of political agenda is evident in the growth of Christianity under its initial duress and harsh persecution in the pagan Roman Empire, growth through the centuries, and growth in the twentieth and twenty-first centuries in dictatorial and totalitarian countries.

7. What are the three reasons the author lists as to why the Founder's central cultural vision is in danger of removal? (404-405)

The Judeo-Christian worldview is in danger of utter removal from American culture because of a loss of an understanding of the uniqueness of its worth, the loss of America's ability to exclude those things which strike at the heart of its central cultural vision, and America's inability to distinguish that which counts for much and that which counts for little.

8. How does the author describe the moral and intellectual bankruptcy of humanism in American culture? (406-407)

Humanism under the labels of modern liberalism and progressivism is morally and intellectually bankrupt. Its policies are ill conceived, incoherent, and have led to high rates of divorce, co-habitation, illegitimacy, abortion, single family households resulting in poverty, and drug abuse to name just a few. The nation has moved toward economic bondage in both government and private sectors as socialism and its entitlement mentality have become ingrained in the American consciousness. There has been a broad and deep coarsening of culture as lewdness, vulgarity, lawlessness, and violence have bled from the entertainment media into the streets and homes of America.

9. In the political and economic arena, what must be done to recapture America's central cultural vision? (407)

In the political and economic arena, there must be election and appointment of officials that understand the roots of the disintegration of American culture and who unswervingly implement policies that adhere to the founding principles under the over-arching banner of the Judeo-Christian ethic.

10. Although the prescriptions in political and economic areas are important, what does the author say is most important for combating the cancer of humanism that has invaded the American cultural vision? (408)

Although political and economic measures are important, ultimate and sustained healing must come from within, not just through the application of Band-Aids to the abrasions caused by modern secular society. Healing must proceed from a re-establishment of order. As we have seen, order allows the establishment of laws that support order. From just laws, justice is made possible, and from the possibility of justice flows freedom.

11. What must happen in America for this order to be achieved? (408)

Order in society can only be achieved from a right ordering of the soul of the individual. This order is achieved as man comes into a proper relationship with God. When individuals collectively order their souls and achieve a proper relationship with God, unity is advanced and the central cultural vision is restored. Here we speak of a moral and spiritual regeneration of America through spiritual renewal, often called a religious revival or awakening, that will set the "…moral tone in opposition to today's liberal relativism." That is the prescription for America. That healing must begin with the individual and a subsequent national spiritual renewal—a remedy that has served America well during several periods of crisis in its colonial and national history.

12. What was the common theme or condition in America preceding each of the three major spiritual renewals during the nation's history and what was the common element that brought about the renewals? (408-413)

The nation generally faced significant and protracted periods of moral decline or spiritual crises prior to each of the spiritual renewals or awakenings. The common element that brought about spiritual renewals was concerted prayer by Christians.

13. What is the ultimate solution for restoration of the Judeo-Christian central cultural vision of America's Founders? (414)

God's response to Solomon's petitions in II Chronicles 7:14 gives the answer: "If my people who are called by my name humble themselves, and pray and seek my face, and turn from their wicked ways, then I will hear from heaven and will forgive their sin and heal their land."

www.ingramcontent.com/pod-product-compliance
Lightning Source LLC
Chambersburg PA
CBHW071556040426
42452CB00008B/1198